CLASS STRUCTURE
& SOCIAL MOBILITY
IN POLAND

CLASS STRUCTURE & SOCIAL MOBILITY IN POLAND

EDITED WITH AN INTRODUCTION BY
KAZIMIERZ SŁOMCZYŃSKI AND TADEUSZ KRAUZE

M. E. SHARPE, INC. WHITE PLAINS, NEW YORK

Translated by Anna M. Furdyna.

Published simultaneously as Vol. VII, no. 3-4 of
International Journal of Sociology

Library of Congress Catalog Card Number: 78-56273
International Standard Book Number: 0-87332-120-0

Printed in the United States of America

CONTENTS

FOREWORD

How far have sociologists working in countries commonly designated as "socialist" gone in studying the class structure and social consciousness of their own societies? What kinds of questions have they posed, and what is the degree of technical sophistication applied in answering them? Western sociologists interested in the fate of their discipline in Eastern Europe and the Soviet Union have long recognized that the answers to these questions will differ substantially depending upon which particular socialist society one has in mind. They would also probably agree that throughout most of the postwar period Polish sociology — in terms of the range of its interests and its general scientific stature — has had few, if any, rivals among the socialist countries. Indeed, it has served as an important catalyst for the legitimation and development of sociology as a distinct social science discipline in other socialist countries, including the Soviet Union.

But it would be an injustice to Polish sociologists to regard the significance of their work solely from the standpoint of its "leading role" among socialist countries. Polish sociologists would undoubtedly want their work appraised in a broader context, and with some justification. One reason for this is suggested by the report of a Western scholar who has followed the development of sociology in Eastern Europe: "In stratification, political sociology, and rural sociology Poland is probably

ahead of a number of West European countries" (Bogdan De-
nitch in Slavic Review, June 1971, p. 233). Whether all ob-
servers would agree with this judgment or not, it does suggest
the need for greater first-hand familiarity with the work of
Polish sociologists.

The selection from Polish sociological literature brought together here by Słomczyński and Krauze should help to answer
the questions we have raised and provide readers with the opportunity to assess the quality of Polish sociological studies in
the areas of class structure, social mobility, and class consciousness. A number of works by Polish sociologists have appeared in English in the postwar period (see, for example, the
selections in R. Bendix and S. M. Lipset, eds., Class, Status
and Power, New York, The Free Press, 1966; A. Béteille, ed.,
Social Inequality, Baltimore, Penguin Books, 1969; International
Journal of Sociology, Winter 1974-75). But the papers which
follow are, to my knowledge, the only collection of Polish materials to appear in recent years that is explicitly focused on
the areas I have specified.

Quite apart from the substantive content of the selections,
readers accustomed to following sociological literature in
various countries will welcome the relative absence of
ideological jargon and of the compulsion to glorify alleged national achievements and the superiority of officially sanctioned
philosophical approaches. The presence or absence of these
compulsions, and the resulting cross-national differences in
the "tone" of sociological discourse, are no small matter. At
the very least they serve as rough indicators of the degree of
maturity — and indeed, security — of sociology as a scientific
discipline.

The studies grouped under the heading "Transformations of
Class Structure" are concerned primarily with identifying and
characterizing the classes, strata, and occupational groups
which emerged from the postwar industrialization process.
This process itself is directed by a particular kind of "industrializing group," one whose political character and ideology
guide strategic decisions in both the economic and social

Foreword

sphere. In this sense "...political institutions are the dominant institutions, and they subordinate all other types of institutions and all fields of endeavor" (Szczepański).

The classes and strata identified in the first section are the
social groups whose sources of recruitment and mobility patterns are analyzed in the papers in the second section. The
conceptual apparatus underlying these empirical studies of social mobility (the distinctions between structural and exchange
mobility, intergenerational and intragenerational mobility)
seems essentially the same as that employed in Western mobility
studies. The common methodology, as well as the abundant detail on the samples studies, should facilitate cross-national
comparisons.

The kinds of issues raised in the studies in the third section
("Class Consciousness and Class Interests") are precisely
those which are largely ignored in the sociological literature of
most socialist countries. Nor are they a principal area of study
in American sociology. Polish sociology, however, seems to
have a well-established tradition of studies of the "subjective"
aspects of class structure based on public opinion surveys.
How do the principal social groups differ in their perceptions
of class structure and the relations between classes? How do
they identify their own class position? How do the value systems of the various social groups differ? Would an income
structure which reflected social groups' conceptions of their
own "adequate" income levels be more, or less, egalitarian than
the prevailing income structure? These are some of the questions bearing on social consciousness posed in these studies.

Our own provisional — and admittedly not very precise —
answer to the question with which we began this note would be
that at least in the case of Poland, sociologists have gone rather
far in exploring the class structure and social consciousness
of their own land. The papers which follow should help readers
to decide for themselves whether to accept or reject our judgment.

Murray Yanowitch

ACKNOWLEDGMENTS

The editors gratefully acknowledge the support of the International Research and Exchanges Board (IREX ad hoc grant and collaborative projects grant during the academic year 1976/77 for T. K.) and the Council for International Exchange of Scholars (CIES grant 78-015-a during the academic year 1977/78 for K. S.).

INTRODUCTION

Kazimierz Słomczyński and Tadeusz Krauze

Studies of class structure and social mobility are among the most highly developed branches of sociology in Poland. This is due to three factors: the national tradition of such studies, the rapid transformation of Polish society after the Second World War, and last, the recent impact of Marxist theory on the social sciences.

In 1920 a research center was established in Warsaw at which the class structure of Polish society was studied intensively. Between 1920 and 1939 it undertook a number of research projects devoted chiefly to the investigation of the standard of living of the working class and peasantry. This research center engaged primarily in empirical surveys. Another research center specialized in collecting and analyzing personal documents, mainly diaries. In retrospect Polish sociology of this period can be regarded as having a strong empirical orientation.

The rapid transformation of Polish society after the Second World War was brought about by the socialist revolution, characterized by the impact of the Workers' Party, the nationalization of industry, agrarian reform, and central planning. In this context new processes within a given class structure and new patterns of social mobility became an object of special attention for sociologists. Class structure and social mobility were considered not only from the point of view of changes in the political and economic system but also with respect to transformations in cultural institutions and the educational system. Formation of the "new society" inspired this research perspective (Szczepański, 1971).

The impact of Marxist theory on the social sciences, already evident in the period from 1918 to 1939, has intensified since 1945. In 1947 Adam Schaff's Introduction to the Theory of Marxism appeared and was widely read and discussed. This book presented an explanation of some specific features of the revolutionary changes in Poland.

Later, discussions of Marx's theory of class were enriched by Ossowski's book Class Structure in the Social Consciousness (1957). However, only after the publication of the works of Julian Hochfeld (1961a, 1961b, 1963) did a research program on class structure crystallize. This crystallization was embedded in the intellectual framework sometimes called "open Marxism," which denotes the application of the foundations of Marxist theory to new problems (Wiatr, 1973). The theme of class structure in a socialist society belongs to this class of problems.

Since the end of the Second World War, the development of empirical research in Polish sociology has been far from uniform. In the years 1945-49 Polish sociology came to life anew after the destruction caused by the war. In view of the drastically reduced number of staff and difficulties with organization, empirical investigations on a large scale were not possible, although a need for them was deeply felt. During the 1950-55 period the political climate did not particularly favor empirical investigation. However, Polish sociologists pointed out that research on the working class was deeply rooted in the Marxist tradition and that it should be introduced without further delay. Consequently, research projects concerning the working class and the intelligentsia were undertaken.

More intensive progress in empirical investigations of class structure, stratification, and social mobility followed after 1955. At first these investigations were concentrated within the confines of the Polish Academy of Sciences. With the passage of time more and more scientific organizations began such investigations, especially the university institutes of sociology.

Introduction

The University of Warsaw, Łódź University, the Jagiellonian
University in Kraków, and the University of Poznań have outstanding institutes of sociology.

Up to 1970 there was little coordination in the work of the
various scientific centers. On the one hand, this encouraged
differentiation of topics and methods, but on the other hand, it
led to relatively meager cumulative findings. At the beginning
of the seventies investigations of social structure and its transformation were approved by the government as one of the most
important areas of sociological study and were awarded increased financial support. Thus arose a need for coordination
of the various research projects, a job entrusted to the Polish
Academy of Sciences. Not only did the Academy have to coor-
dinate the topics of projects in progress, but it also had to suggest some methods for investigative procedures. During the
five-year period 1975-79 more than fifty projects are to be co-
ordinated by the Academy.

One of the basic indicators of the development of a specialty
is the number of publications on it. In Poland the number of
sociological papers on class structure and mobility currently
exceeds 150 per annum, while fifteen years ago it was less
than fifty.

The contributions selected for this volume are not limited to
articles from journals but also include excerpts from books,
since different ways of presenting and interpreting empirical
data are displayed in various types of sources.

The present volume consists of three parts. In the first,
three papers by Szczepański, Wesołowski, and Zagórski, respectively, describe the general transformations of class structure in a historical framework. The paper by Szczepański is
an excerpt from his book about the process of industrialization
in Poland during the years 1945-70. The author considers the
qualitative and quantitative changes in class structure in different phases of development of the political and economic system.

This range of problems is extended in the paper by Wesołowski, who also considers the technological-economic and the
historical-cultural contexts as determinants of social classes

3

and socioeconomic groups. The essay by Zagórski provides
basic data about the size and internal composition of these
groups and thus constitutes a useful background for the other
papers.

The second part of this volume is devoted to social mobility.
Another paper by Zagórski, which presents the results of a
survey of over 70,000 persons, is followed by an article by
Janicka based on more intensive analysis of data obtained from
smaller surveys. These two essays analyze intergenerational
mobility, while the remaining one, by Słomczyński, pertains to
intragenerational mobility. While all the papers in this section
of the volume reveal, directly or indirectly, the role of education as a factor explaining the flow of persons between occupations, the last piece focuses on it.

The third part of the volume pertains to class consciousness
and class interests. The papers in this section discuss not only
such classical problems as the common image of class structure (Malanowski) and perceptions of the adequacy of incomes
(Szafnicki) but also new problems, e.g., the place of power
among the socially desired values (Koralewicz-Zębik). One
essay (Ostrowski) does not pertain to consciousness but to behavior: its purpose is to explore the participation of workers
who hold various levels of offices in the trade unions.

The papers selected were written in a country where sociologists are accustomed to viewing class structure as a phenomenon different from social stratification. This distinction as
applied to a socialist society has been developed by Wesołowski
(1966) and is shared by a large number of sociologists in Poland. The theoretical basis of this view will be presented below, since it may help readers correctly understand the papers.

Taking as a point of departure the Marxist theory of social
change, Polish sociologists attempt to show that in this theory
classes are defined primarily through economic dominance,
which in turn implies their specific political and ideological
functions in society. According to this interpretation classes
are distinguished on the basis of certain relations rather than
attributes, and they are considered as social groups with their

4

own history. In Marxist theory the relation to the means of
production is considered fundamental because it determines
many other social relations.

The working class, the intelligentsia, and the peasantry are
usually distinguished in the class structure of a socialist society. Certain more detailed classifications also include artisans (small private producers) and, within the intelligentsia,
white-collar workers. These categories may be considered
segments of the class structure because their members have a
different degree of control over the means of production, the
process of work, and the final product. This differing degree
of control affects the position of individuals in dominance-
subordination relations in the political and ideological spheres.

These large social groups emerged in the previous socioeconomic epoch. In Poland, however, since the Second World War
the functions of these groups have changed fundamentally. In
the new political situation the working class, the intelligentsia,
and the peasants have gradually lost their class characteristics,
paralleling the development of the socialist state. In particular, the control of the economy by the state through central
planning has diminished the importance of the definitional distinction involving the relation to the means of production. This
suggests that the classes distinguished by Marxist theory are
former classes rather than classes that exist at present. According to such an interpretation social classes in the socialist
state should be considered remnants of the previous socioeconomic period.

This class heritage is relatively durable, however. In Poland
the peasants own their own farms and are involved in traditional
social relations typical of small communities. The intelligentsia often exhibits internal solidarity in defense of its special
interests. While the socialist revolution has eliminated the
foundations of the old class structure, some of its characteristics remain.

A focal point of interest is the relationship between the class
structure and the stratification system. By stratification we
mean the existence of social aggregates distinguished by in-

equalities in the sharing of generally desired goods. In this approach the main dimensions of stratification are income, standard of living, consumption of cultural goods, and prestige.

According to Marxist theory the stratification system is determined, in the statistical sense, by class structure. In a socialist society class differences gradually disappear, but stratification differences are necessary for the functioning of this type of society. Proceeding from the general hypothesis that the changed distribution of goods is to a large extent independent of inherited class structure, Polish sociologists search for other factors that determine stratification.

The division of labor is seen as the most important of these factors, particularly socio-occupational differentiation. In the Marxist theory of the emergence and development of capitalism, the individual's position in the division of labor is the intervening variable between his class position and his social status. Since in socialist society class structure is in the process of disappearing, while the division of labor is not, one should expect the division of labor to determine the distributional (stratification) differences. The treatment of occupation as a strategic variable in research on inequality is reflected in the papers included in this volume.

The data used by the authors were collected mainly during the period 1967-72. Since then many new data have been collected, analyzed, and interpreted. The conclusions that have been reached, however, are similar to those presented in this volume. This can be seen clearly, for example, in a paper (Wesołowski and Słomczyński, 1977) that presents the results of surveys conducted during 1965-67 and 1976 in Łódź, a city of 500,000 inhabitants. The ranking of occupational groups with respect to average education, income, standard of living, and level of cultural participation is almost identical in the two time periods. The top positions are occupied by professionals, followed by technicians and office workers. The middle positions are held by foremen, service workers, and skilled factory workers. At the bottom are semiskilled and unskilled factory workers.

Introduction

The range of the hierarchy has not changed appreciably. For example, during both time periods professional earned approximately twice as much as unskilled factory workers. Correlations between income, education, standard of living, and cultural consumption also turn out to be stable.

The absence of basic changes in class structure and social mobility in Poland over the last five years justifies the inclusion in this volume of results that are not brand new but are a part of the achievements of Polish sociology. Generally the quality of data is high, a fact which should encourage international comparisons.

References

Hochfeld, Julian.
    1961a. "Marksowska teoria klas: próba systematyzacji. Część I" [Marx's theory of class: an attempt at systematization. Part I]. Studia Socjologiczne 1.
    1961b. "Marksowska teoria klas: próba systematyzacji. Część II" [Marx's theory of class: an attempt at systematization. Part II]. Studia Socjologiczne 3.
    1963. Studia o Marksowskiej teorii społeczeństwa [Studies on Marx's theory of society]. Warsaw: Państwowe Wydawnictwo Naukowe.
Ossowski, Stanisław.
    1957. Struktura klasowa w społecznej świadomości [Class structure in the social consciousness]. Łódź: Państwowe Wydawnictwo Naukowe.
Schaff, Adam.
    1947. Wstęp do teorii marksizmu [Introduction to the theory of Marxism]. Warsaw: Książka i Wiedza.
Szczepański, Jan.
    1971. Odmiany czasu teraźniejszego [Present-day transformation]. Warsaw: Książka i Wiedza.
    1973. Zmiany społeczeństwa polskiego w procesie uprzemysłowienia [Changes in Polish society during the process of industrialization]. Warsaw: Instytut Wydawniczy Centralnej Rady Związków Zawodowych.

Wesołowski, Włodzimierz.
   1966.   Klasy, warstwy i władza [Classes, strata, and power].
            Warsaw: Państwowe Wydawnictwo Naukowe.
Wesołowski, Włodzimierz, and Słomczyński, Kazimierz.
   1977.   "Przemiany struktury społecznej i jej potocznej percepcji"
            [Changes in social structure and its common image]. Pa-
            per presented at the Congress of the Polish Sociological
            Association. Kraków, January.
Wiatr, Jerzy.
   1973.   "Juliana Hochfelda marksizm otwarty" [The open Marxism
            of Julian Hochfeld]. Studia Socjologiczne 4. 103-19.

PART ONE

Transformations of Class Structure

Jan Szczepański

EARLY STAGES OF SOCIALIST INDUSTRIALIZATION AND CHANGES IN SOCIAL CLASS STRUCTURE*

Properties of Socialist Industrialization

On what does the difference between socialist industrialization and other historically known types of industrialization depend? Technologically there are no basic differences. The technical knowledge with which industrial plants and other facilities are built is the common property of the epoch; it is international in character. Needless to say, specific technical solutions can be different in different countries; certain advanced technologies can be the secret property of states or industrial concerns, etc. In principle, however, technological variations are secondary.

The complex of economic processes and characteristics is primary, however. A socialist economy is one in which social appropriation of the means of production has taken place, and one with a planned, centralized economy directed and administered by the government. Therefore in the course of industrial expansion, the economic system functions in an entirely different way than an economic system arising in the course of capitalist industrialization. The characteristic trait of socialist

---

*From Jan Szczepański, Zmiany społeczeństwa polskiego w procesie uprzemysłowienia (Warsaw: Instytut Wydawniczy Centralnej Rady Związków Zawodowych, 1973), pp. 18-22, 24, 46-48, 100-214, 230-48, 275-83. Abridgements and editorial changes were introduced by the editors with the author's consent.

industrialization is the coupling of the economic and political systems, and therefore its sociological aspects are extremely interesting and important. In a number of postcapitalist countries, nationalization of the economy has taken place to some extent, and planning has embraced increasing areas of the economy. This, however, does not bring their economic models closer to the model instituted in Eastern European countries. The difference lies primarily in the importance of social and political factors in management and administration, and this results in concrete differences in the functioning of the economy.

The groups that direct socialist industrialization and make strategic decisions arise from a political party of the Marxist-Leninist type. The basis of these groups' actions is the sociopolitical doctrine of the party. The party also creates an ideology that justifies and directs the economic policy. Kerr and his coauthors saw in the nature of the industrializing group a characteristic that typifies socialist industrialization.[1] The political character of this group, its ideology and its aims, and the subordination of technological and economic goals of industrialization to political necessities undoubtedly affect in a decisive way the economic model formed during the course of expansion.

The most important social and economic characteristic of socialist industrialization, however, is the model of the enterprise. I would be inclined to say that the model of the enterprise determines the essential differences between socialist and other types of industrialization. It is defined by the party ideology. It is a nationalized enterprise (or more accurately, a socialized one in which there is no private owner) in which the workers are "socialist co-owners" and, through the institution of self-government, have some influence on managerial decisions. Such an enterprise is a constitutive institution of the new socialist society. Building the socialist economy, a planned economy working to meet the needs of the entire population, is the goal of industrialization. Every factory and firm, as well as every institution, must be incorporated without conflict into the general model, the function of which is to create

the proper macro- and microstructure of socialist society.
Therefore ideological goals cannot be subjugated to an economic
or technical rationale, as is the case in other types of industrialization. Whereas ideology plays an auxiliary role in justifying
the methods used in other types of industrialization, in this case
the ideology of the group directing industrialization is a principal and determining value.

Socialist industrialization means the expansion of industry —
the essential factor in the growth of a nationalized and planned
economy — in accord with the ideological vision of a socialist
society, defined by the principles of Marxism-Leninism. Socialist industrialization not only changes the structure of the
economy but also aims to accelerate economic growth, measured by economic criteria, and to create a new socialist base
from which can be erected, through government planning, a new
social system. For this reason, with respect to all economic
theories and definitions of socialist industrialization, I think
that a complete picture can be obtained only by an examination
of its social aspects.[2]

Early Stages of Socialist Industrialization

The stage of national industrialization is the period in which
industry as a whole requires decisions about changing the structure of productive investment. This means that in differentiating the early stages we will have to consider economic as well
as technical phenomena to a much greater extent. I want to
emphasize strongly that in this discussion we are not interested
in technical and economic changes per se but only in their social aspects, i.e., the social phenomena and processes that necessarily accompany them.

Taking these considerations into account, let us outline the
stages of industrialization for the country as a whole:

1) The preliminary stage consisted primarily of reaching a
state of economic growth allowing the initiation of productive
investments on a broad scale. In Poland this was a period of

reconstruction from the damage of war and of preparing industry, its workers, and the planning and administrative apparatus
for beginning the six-year plan. This first phase ended in 1949.

2) The second phase was one of basic investments, primarily
in heavy industry producing the means of production. This
phase coincided approximately with the duration of the six-year
plan (1950-55) and continued through the first years of the following five-year plan (1956-60). This does not mean that investments in heavy industry ended in those years, but during
the period they were the dominant, most important investments
on which the main effort was concentrated. Of the more than
100 enterprises constructed during the six-year plan, investments in mines, mills, cement factories, machinery plants, and
the chemical industry definitely exceeded investments in light
industry and food production.

3) The third phase of Poland's industrialization began with a
revision of plans for the years 1956-57 and then was given final
form in the outline of the next five-year plan, 1961-65. This
phase may be called the complementary phase. On the one hand,
industrial investment expenditures were considerably reduced
as a proportion of total investment (from 38.7% in the years
1956-60 to 27.7% in the years 1961-65), and on the other hand,
the funding for light industry and food processing increased as
a proportion of industrial growth itself. This was a consequence
of the simple principle of complementarity in industry as a
whole or the division of labor among the branches of industry.
Unbalanced industry cannot develop properly unless it is based
on well-functioning international cooperation. Thus the pressure of technical necessities and of the population's consumer
needs resulted in the decision to initiate productive investments
in a wider range of industries and in those sectors of the economy which, for various reasons, had been less developed in the
previous period.

The Preliminary Stage

In this discussion we will adopt a class theory in which the

14

definition of class is based on relation to the means of production, the share of income received, and place in the production process. But we shall add to these the opportunities and lifestyle that develop in families and social circles. Therefore to describe and explain changes in classes and social strata we have to go beyond the composition of the work force and the training and attitudes required in the work place.

In the liberated territories in 1944-45 there was a natural tendency to re-create and reconstruct the prewar social structure. This impulse was natural because a different social system was known only from ideals and ideologies, whereas the prewar social structure was remembered and had shaped people's life experience. Although it is true that war and occupation destroyed this structure, and moreover, that during the years of occupation it was discredited as a result of the September defeat, the behavior patterns stemming from it persisted.

The prewar system of classes and strata included the following groups:

1) The large landowners, a class historically enjoying the highest prestige and possessing over 27% of the land, thus making hundreds and thousands of people dependent on it either directly or indirectly.

2) The bourgeoisie, or the owners of large and middle-sized industrial, service, and financial enterprises. Next to the large landowners, it was the richest class, and thus it also had the best opportunities and the greatest political influence.

3) Next in the social hierarchy was the intelligentsia, or the educated population, which traditionally had exercised cultural leadership in the nation throughout the nineteenth century. In the period before the war, the intelligentsia was composed of various categories of intellectuals, professional people, white-collar workers, teachers, and the lower ranks of administrative office workers.

4) It is necessary to mention the petite bourgeoisie, or the owners of small industrial, artisan, and trade enterprises, etc. It was a rather varied class in which one should also include

both the affluent owners of prospering enterprises and travel-
ing salesmen.

5) The peasant class, internally divided into several strata,
was the largest group in the prewar period. The peasants had
existed as far back in the country's history as the large landowners, but they did not hold a position proportionate either to
their numbers and traditions or to their contribution to the life
of the nation.

6) The working class was not very large because of the lack
of industrial development, but it played an important political
role in the country.

7) The agricultural workers, the lowest category of the rural
proletariat, earned the lowest wages and had the fewest opportunities.

8) Marginal elements were the lumpen proletariat, idle itin-
erants, beggars, and the chronically unemployed.

This class-stratum structure was largely destroyed by the
war. Displacements and confiscations considerably weakened
the landowners. The appropriation of factories and the absorp-
tion of the Polish economy into the German war effort undermined the Polish bourgeoisie and petite bourgeoisie. Moreover,
the barbarous extermination of the Jewish population totally
changed its composition. The intelligentsia was the object of
particularly fierce repression, for it was feared as a managerial and leadership force. Thus the losses were enormous,
especially in the category of those having higher education.
The peasant and working classes suffered relatively least, although they were also affected by deportation and repression
for participating in the resistance movement. The war and occupation changed the previously established lifestyles, patterns,
and behavior and value systems of all classes. Above all, however, a great "shuffling" took place. Higher classes were deprived
of the means of performing ordinary work. The intelligentsia, ex-
pelled from the liquidated institutions, looked for other means of
survival and took up such jobs as service work, etc. The same can
be said of the large landowners and bourgeoisie. The petite bourgeoisie, deprived of its workshops, survived by either semi-

legal or totally illegal operations, thus taking advantage of flaws
and gaps in the German economy. During this period a mass
phenomenon of "making it on the side" began, one which persisted long after the end of the war.

In the years 1944-45 masses of people returning from all
parts of the world, from prisoner-of-war and concentration
camps, from deportation and compulsory labor, from emigra-
tion and also from displacement to the General Province, attempted not only to return to their places in the geographic
sense but also to their social positions and to the prewar lifestyle that seemed "normal" to them. If they settled in another
town, they tried to regain their occupations, their prewar social
position and lifestyle. Thus there existed a general tendency
to "re-create" the prewar social structure.

This tendency was modified, however, by extremely powerful
factors. The war losses created large gaps and, therefore, the
need to replace people in managerial and other professional
positions, for these categories had been especially persecuted
by the occupying forces and had sustained the greatest losses.
The door to advancement was opened for those who could replace them. The new system created new types of institutions
and opportunities. Socialist and democratic ideology initiated
social status criteria that were unknown before the war. Finally, such social reforms as the land reform, the expropriation
of former German abandoned estates and enterprises, and the
nationalization of industry were factors that considerably modified the tendency to rebuild the prewar social structure.

As a result, during this period the classes that were most
affluent and influential before the war, that is, the large landowners and the bourgeoisie, were eliminated. The economic
bases for the existence of these classes were taken over by the
state or, in the case of agricultural estates, divided among the
peasants and farm workers. The large landowning class did
not regenerate, since land reform was carried out immediately
after the liberation of Polish territories and advanced with the
war front.

The bourgeoisie had some potential for rebirth even after

17

nationalization, which affected only private enterprises employing more than fifty workers. In 1947 there were 172,522 private industrial and artisan enterprises in Poland, of which 152,646 employed fewer than five workers. From this it appears that 19,876 businesses employed more workers, and to some extent they can be considered the base for the existence of a capitalist class. In the same year 123,092 private trade establishments and 27,862 service trade establishments existed, but it is difficult to say if they should be considered an economic base for the capitalist class. In any case, in contrast to the large landowners, a bourgeoisie continued to exist, although it is clear that it neither regained its prewar affluence nor possessed its former political influence. It was totally excluded from positions of power; and after a few years, when smaller industrial merchant and other service establishments were also nationalized, it disappeared as a class.

The fate of the petite bourgeoisie was closely tied to that of the large landowners and the bourgeoisie. This class could not regenerate itself in its prewar form, since a large portion of it had perished during the conflict. Thus it was reborn with an entirely different composition, made up largely of people who found their livelihood in random sources of income. The petite bourgeoisie was an extremely fluid class during this period, and many people belonged to it who lived in semilegal conditions, in a state of constant insecurity and anxiety.

The intelligentsia emerged from the war almost totally destroyed. A great proportion of the educated people were killed, many emigrants did not return, and many lost their health. The work places of the intelligentsia had been demolished, and the influx of new members was retarded due to the closing of schools by the occupying forces. And yet the decisive role in the process of reconstruction and building of the economy fell to this group.

We must emphasize several points about the rebirth of the intelligentsia.

1) The system of people's democracy, a grass-roots form of proletarian dictatorship, advocated a new concept of people's

intelligentsia, i.e., an intelligentsia deriving from the manual laboring classes, tied to these classes by a familial bond, by a feeling of identity, and by a resulting acceptance of socialist ideology as the ideology of these classes.

2) The functions of the intelligentsia in this system were defined as professional, and the intelligentsia itself was defined as a stratum of highly qualified white-collar workers. This is an especially important point for the future industrialization process, since even in this first period the development of technical studies and professional education was stressed. In any case, this idea did not meet with approval by the working and peasant classes.

3) In order to accelerate the processes of training working-class and peasant youth and of opening higher education to them, so-called preparatory courses were created. These courses were organized in 1946-47 and continued for a long time afterwards. The objective of these courses was to make college attendance possible for the talented and motivated peasant and working-class youth who had not been able to finish secondary school. Abridged technical courses were also created for "advanced workers," i.e., for workers marked by occupational qualifications, intelligence, and imagination.

4) At the same time, outstanding workers and peasants were promoted to leadership and white-collar positions in an effort to advance them in industry and, above all, in political institutions, i.e., in the party apparatus and the country's administration. The shifting of workers to leadership and managerial positions in industry began on a larger scale in 1949.

5) Among the growing number of students in secondary schools and colleges, an increasing percentage of places was reserved for the children of peasant and worker families, with the aim of changing the social composition of the intelligentsia through the normal course of schooling. Slowly at first, but with increasingly wider scope, social programs were geared to political and ideological education in order to achieve the desired identification of the intelligentsia with the aims and ideologies of the socialist system. This process began in 1944-45.

All these ways of forming the intelligentsia had one goal: to
create a stratum of highly qualified white-collar workers who
would implement the party's plans for the construction of the
new system based on a socialized economy and, above all, on a
socialized industry. The years 1944-49 constituted a period of
consolidation of power. It was evident for the group wielding
authority that the decisive importance in this process lay in the
reconstruction of the economy and in assuring the fulfillment
of needs and opportunities for the population. The vision of the
future, in the name of which the battle to establish popular rule
was fought, was a vision of an industrialized, affluent society
in which everyone would have equal opportunities in life. In the
name of this vision, which can only be realized by a popular
government, the ideal model of the white-collar worker was
created, and an appeal was made to the imagination and patrio-
tism of the intelligentsia.

Considerable changes also took place in the working class.
Its position in society was altered. Together with the nationalization of industry, with the institution of worker's councils,
and with the granting of political and economic rights to labor
unions, the workers became comanagers of industrial plants.
Their position in the technical system of factories, which resulted from the relationship of worker to machine, did not
change, nor did their place in the division of labor, for they
still remained hired laborers. But their legal status in relation
to their employer was changed.

On the other hand, the composition of the working class began
to change due to its political function. It was the fundamental
class in the system of people's democracy. The participation
of the workers in the formation of the power system was very
great during this period. In practice this meant that thousands
of workers moved from work in shops in the production plant
to desk jobs: in labor unions, in the party apparatus, in the national administration, in economic institutions, and in industrial
management.

During this period a process with deep repercussions took
place — the "self-recruitment of the working class." Before

the war, because of the major difficulties entailed in attending
secondary schools, the ordinary way of life for a working-class
child was to enter the factory where his father worked. The
lifestyle of the family, a style peculiar to the working class, was
determined, among other things, by the range of career possibilities. The development of the school system, the creation of
institutes of accelerated education, and the securing of over
30% of all places in secondary and higher schools for working-
class children provided exit routes from working-class occupations. Working-class youth were highly motivated to attend
academic secondary schools, since these schools were the established symbol of the way up the social ladder before the war.
The old ideal of social advancement was acquiring new possibilities for its realization.

Working-class culture also began to change through the dissemination of newspapers, books, radio, and various kinds of
educational programs, ideological training, popularization of
science, etc. Although studies conducted toward the end of the
fifties found that this process was a slow one, its beginnings go
back to the first years after the war. Two processes began that
reached a decisive stage around 1965: the adaptation of old
workers who were already working before the war, and the en-
trance of new workers into the working class. The old workers
were socialized by the capitalist factory and its labor relations,
by the class struggle that went on inside it, and by workers'
institutions organized to lead it. Class consciousness was
formed through opposition to the capitalists and on the basis of
an acute awareness of opposing interests. Around 1965 the process began of entering working-class occupations through the
educational system. Working-class consciousness was shaped
by worker organizations established to implement government
plans that considered the long-range interests of the whole society. For both the old and the new workers this situation led
to many doubts and misunderstandings. Hence the importance
of adaptation processes that began in the first phase of industrialization.

The most considerable changes in this period took place in

the peasant class. The contributing factors were: land reform and the division of land tracts among the agricultural workers and peasants; the migration to the western territories and the settlement program in these territories; the migration of the rural population to the cities, particularly settling in cities completely demolished during the war and in small towns in which the population was displaced or was exterminated during the occupation; the settling in deserted towns and cities in the western and northern territories; the access to secondary and higher education and the emergence of secondary schools in villages; transfer to jobs in other sectors of the economy while continuing work on the farm; the rise of the average educational level, the widening scope of rural education, the increased penetration of cultural media to villages; the rise in the standard of living and the elimination of rural overpopulation.

Despite these changes, in the initial period the peasant class began to be reconstituted in keeping with the prewar image of the peasant's situation. Soon, however, the results of concrete changes appeared. The landowner's estate, the real agent which shaped social relations in the village, disappeared from the countryside. The hopeless proletariat of landless peasants vanished, and the previous status of peasants on decrepit and small farms was altered. Resettling and migration to cities relieved the overpopulation of the villages. The school system created opportunities for the peasant youth to move into nonagrarian trades. The peasants who remained in the villages had to adapt themselves to these changes, that is, to alter their traditional methods of farming. In this way the foundations were laid for the turns entailed in the next stage of industrialization. These changes were redirected for a few years, however, by a radically new course of agricultural policy initiated in 1949-50.

The class of agricultural workers dwindled drastically during this time. An appreciable proportion of the old agricultural workers obtained their own farms. The difficulties of managing them, however, produced a situation in which these new farmers were becoming potential candidates for the status of farmer-workers. A sizeable proportion of agricultural workers moved to the cities; the rest transferred to jobs on farms under government management, from which the state agricultural farms would be formed in the future.

Similarly, the traditional types of the beggar, the idle itinerant, and the unemployed have disappeared. On the other hand, immediately after the war there were an immense number of orphans, cripples, and homeless individuals roaming the country in search of their families and the possibility of finding a home. These multitudes of people, estimated in the hundreds of thousands, were included in the "social rescue" action that attempted to create opportunities for them.

Summarizing the changes in the class and stratum structure we can note the following: the disappearance of upper classes, the total transformation of the petite bourgeoisie, changes in the composition of the intelligentsia, and the beginning of reorganization processes in the working and peasant classes.

The Period of Basic Industrialization

In the period of basic industrialization the traditional classes and strata underwent further transformation. Despite the ideological proclamation that announced the emergence of new classes and strata appropriate to a socialist society, in reality the process could take place only after the construction of a new socialized economy and after the stabilization of the political and administrative institutions of the new state. During the period of the six-year plan both were merely in formative stages. Industrialization and the simultaneous process of creating a socialist state, however, were extremely powerful factors in changing the composition and nature of traditional social classes and strata.

At the beginning of the six-year plan, Polish society was composed of four basic classes and strata: the working class, the intelligentsia, the peasant class, and the petite bourgeoisie. Let us stress that the petite bourgeoisie was already reduced in size.

Jan Szczepański

Two and a half million workers were added to the increasing ranks of manual laborers in the years between 1949 and 1956. This fact is extremely significant; but even more important than the quantitative growth of the working class was the change in its composition, the generational change, and the entry of young people into industry. During the period 1950-55 the rise of the "new working class" began in Poland. In this process a decisive role was played by vocational training schools, socialized enterprises with their characteristic labor relations, the labor unions which were a part of the power structure, and the changed social status of the worker.

After 1956 generational exchanges in the labor force intensified. Young people came to work, and the percentage of workers trained in trade schools constantly increased. The influence of old workers who remembered the prewar organization of labor and prewar factory social relations decreased.

Workers' councils, according to prevailing ideals, were organized to implement the ideal that the worker is co-owner of the industrial plant and participates in its management. The new personal and social model of the worker defined him as an active producer and participant in management and the implementation of the economic and noneconomic role of the work place.

After 1956 a greater emphasis was placed on vocational preparation, quality of work, efficiency, and involvement of workers — workers' activity. These innovations proceeded along with changes in management and with the granting of a slightly greater freedom of action to the production units. However, the hopes associated with the new model of socialist economy and with the activity of the Economic Council were not fully realized.

Most important during this period was the integration of diverse elements in places of work, voluntary organizations, and new housing projects. The goal was to create new workers who adhered to the model promoted by political organizations and who were heroes of labor, building the new system and devoting their lives to achieve a better future. But the lowering of living

24

standards, the worsening of relations between the leadership
and the workers, the bureaucratization of the work place, and
a lack of understanding of the true desires of the workers ob-
scured the successes of construction, the opening of new factories, and the rise in production indicated by the statistics.
Integration of the working class on the basis of the postulated
model was not successful, and in 1955-56 a crisis was precipi-
tated by the political events related to the Twentieth Congress
of the CPSU (Communist Party of the Soviet Union) and the criticism of the "cult of personality." The Poznań incidents were
a turning point in this process, and during the "Polish October"
the Eighth Plenary Council of the Central Committee of the
PZPR (Polish United Workers' Party) sanctioned a general political change of direction, also manifested in the development
processes of the working class.

Comparing the transformations that occurred in the working
class during the six-year plan to those that occurred in 1944-
49, we can see that changes began to be shaped by the mechanisms of industrialization. Previously, political changes of a
systemic nature were important, but in this period both technical changes (i.e., all those processes we described in industrialized regions) and the political ideology of industrialization
dominated.

A social class is not only formed through work institutions,
however. Processes occurring in family life and leisure time
are also of great importance. The attrition of the traditional
patriarchial family began because work outside the home was
changing the position of the woman in the family. Among textile
workers, where employment of women was always high, these
changes were not felt as acutely as in mining and steel-mill
families, for example, or the families of old, highly skilled
workers in the machine industry.

The increased social and political activity of the workers,
political programs, ideological training, radio, films, and the
extensive dissemination of learning materials exerted a strong
influence on family life and on the entire working class. This
was not yet a mass culture of the type that began developing in

the sixties, but nonetheless a process whereby society would
be reeducated had begun. This method aimed at achieving an
internal integration of the working class. The goal was to produce a group consciousness that would be the basis for uniform
ways of thinking and acting and of realizing the aims outlined
in the central plan. It was also the period of the birth of a new
concept of cultural revolution.[3]

During the six-year plan, under the influence of a theory of
the role of ideology in cultural revolution, stress was laid on
organizing access to the cultural domain for the hitherto deprived classes and strata. Although the theory of socialist re-
alism was a serious attempt to create new cultural values for
the new epoch, it soon merely idealized reality. In the cultural
revolution, on the other hand, the distribution of books, films,
newspapers, and magazines to large masses of the public was
a significant factor. This process was augmented by making
the school system universal and extending instruction to large
numbers of adults. Still, not all the projected aims of this program were achieved. Mass culture and the rapid rise in the
cultural level of the population had to be bolstered by an economic base that would support a correspondingly rapid growth
in the standard of living. The inadequacy of the base impeded
the effectiveness of the cultural revolution. In spite of this the
revolution was a major influence, since it confirmed the feeling
among the workers that they were the fundamental social class,
that great responsibility rested on them, and that they were the
class which decided the outcome of the industrialization process.

The period of fundamental industrialization also transformed
the status and the social character of the intelligentsia. The
following factors contributed to the transformation:

1) the concept of a people's intelligentsia and a socialist intelligentsia, associated with an intensification of class conflict
in the area of ideology;

2) a change in social functions and a strong emphasis on occupational responsibility, expressed in the educational system
and instructional programs;

3) the bureaucratization of the socialist state and the socialized economy;

45566

4) the emerging scientific-technical revolution and, consequently, the increased importance of research workers and
technicians in economic life;

5) the political crisis of Stalinism and the role of the intelligentsia in it.

The idea of a people's intelligentsia assumed that it is a stratum of highly qualified workers performing professional tasks
and ideologically tied to the party. It was hypothesized that
members of the intelligentsia should be recruited from the laboring classes, for then they would have a natural tendency to
accept an ideology expressing the true interests of these classes
and thus would identify their life goals with the goals of the socialist system.

This type of intelligentsia was to be trained in various types
of schools. During the six-year plan, and especially toward its
end, special forms of training for peasants and workers that
had been developed during the three-year plan were considerably curtailed because the school system was already assuring
the proper education of all youth. Institutions of higher learning
and secondary schools were the most important factors in the
recruitment of the new intelligentsia during this stage. Toward
the end of the six-year plan, the number of new graduates from
institutions of higher learning considerably exceeded the number of graduates from these schools during the years between
the wars. During this period about 85,000 students graduated
from schools of higher learning, whereas in 1949-55 the number was 144,496.

During the six-year plan, when the idea of planning was just
taking hold, when the theory of administrative planning was
dominant, and when an attempt was made to match hard technical-economic realities with ideology, the economic role of the
intelligentsia in the progress of a planned system was over-
looked. This was related to the belief that the party was the
sole factor moving the society. The intelligentsia was only supposed to be a group of qualified specialists implementing technical ideas designed by the party management. Engineers were
to be "production officers" carrying out the decisions of head-
quarters; writers were to be "engineers of human souls" re-

shaping them in accordance with the general party line.

The intelligentsia was involved in various forms of sociopolitical activity during this period. Ideologically it was subservient to the ruling working class, but technically the management of the economy was largely in its hands. The technological development of industry also depended on it. Various intelligentsia groups shaped the youth and the nation's cultural values. To fully understand its influence on public life, the following characteristics of the intelligentsia and its internal differentiation should be stressed:

a) The professional differentiation stemming from the progress of knowledge and increasing specialization had consequences for the occupational structure, the formation of professional organizations, and the internal integration of the whole stratum. At that time the growth in importance of professions within the intelligentsia and the division into specialized groups that were gradually transformed into interest groups were increasing.

b) Differentiation of education level (that is, intelligentsia with higher education, with secondary education, and with insufficient education) created either solidarity or antagonism in work places, particularly when such differentiation coincided with differentiation of positions held. In this period some workers with insufficient education, but with strong ideological ties to the party, were promoted to managerial and administrative positions, and they played an important role both in political and economic organizations.

c) There was also functional differentiation in a broad sense, that is, a creative intelligentsia including artists, writers, musicians, and other contributers to esthetic values; a scientific and technical intelligentsia, which began to increase rapidly in this period; verbal technicians, such as journalists, propaganda workers, agitators, popularizers of learning, etc.; political, economic, and administrative managers, whose members steadily increased in conjunction with the growth of the government and the growing bureaucratization of the planning and management of the economy.

28

Socialist Industrialization and Class Structure

In this differentiated stratum the intellectuals and journalists
performed special functions. It was their task to describe and
analyze the new society. But when researchers apply objective
scientific methods to the description of social conditions, they
can easily become critics of these conditions. In 1954 and 1956
the economic difficulties arising from realization of the plan
and unfulfilled expectations, the regimentation of intellectual
and artistic life, the limitations on expressing opinions, and the
growing dissatisfaction in the country were all reflected in the
critical stances of these members of the intelligentsia. Social
criticism is a valid function of a creative intelligentsia, and it
can never be totally redirected into an apologist's role. The
political crisis in the international communist movement after
the Twentieth Congress of the CPSU also elicited a sharp response from the intelligentsia, especially among the young people who had been educated in the spirit of revolutionary ideals,
who had compared reality to the ideological picture of socialism obtained in colleges, and who were becoming ardent propo-
nents of "mending" the socialist system. In this movement
there was no tendency to a return to the prewar status quo. Ac-
cepting the socialist system, the intelligentsia only wanted to
bring it into line with the fundamental ideas of classical Marxism and to cleanse it of Stalinist distortions. I believe that it
is the October period which best showed how far the changes in
the Polish intelligentsia had progressed.

The five-year phase of basic industrialization thoroughly altered the image and character of the peasants. They were differentiated into these categories:

1) peasants who farmed individually and supported themselves solely by work on the farm;

2) peasants working in farming cooperatives, a category created by the collectivization of agriculture;

3) white-collar farmer-workers who contributed their land
to the cooperatives and then sought additional work outside agriculture as white-collar workers in village councils, in cooperatives, and on the railroads;

4) blue-collar farmer-workers, whose members increased

because of industrialization.

It is estimated that from 1946 to 1960 over 2.5 million rural people migrated to the cities. The blurring of social differences through downward mobility also began. The long period of basic industrialization after the political transformation in 1956 accelerated the process already evident during the period of the six-year plan, which B. Gałęski described as the transformation of the peasant class into the occupational category of farmers. Metaphorically, the six-year plan was the mill that shattered the traditional structure of the peasant stratum, eliminated the old ruling authority of the affluent peasant from country life, destroyed the prestige system based solely on acres owned, undermined the remaining traditions of the village community, and created new conditions hampered neither by tradition nor old sources of authority. Although the attempt at collectivization failed, the changes produced by it destroyed the fiber of the traditional peasantry.

In 1944-49 there were many significant changes produced by land reform, by settling of the northern and western territories, by migration to the cities, etc. The essence of the peasant class, however, did not undergo change at this time. Neither the lifestyle, the behavior patterns, the value system, the sources of prestige and hierarchy in the village society, nor the base of authority changed. The period of the six-year plan and the radical stance in relation to class conflict in the country (though not introducing real changes in the agrarian structure or in farming methods, etc.) transformed the organizational ties within this class, the source of prestige, behavior patterns, social values, and aspirations. In this way the basic means for accelerating the transformation of the traditional peasant into a modern farmer were prepared. Such change was long and unsuccessfully fought for from 1919 to 1939, but it was blocked by the traditional structure of society and rural culture. Although the goal of collectivization was not achieved, this period prepared the ground for a very important process that could not have been accomplished under capitalist development, namely, the creation of a modern farming occupation in Poland.

Socialist Industrialization and Class Structure

Migration from villages to towns and the transformations occurring in the peasantry exerted an important influence on other
classes, particularly the working class. A high percentage of
new workers, especially in recently industrialized regions, was
of peasant origins. The rapid development of farmer-workers
constituted the second aspect of "peasantizing" the working
class. During this period a by-product of collectivization also
occurred, i.e., rapid growth in the number of white-collar peasant-workers. This was the result of two tendencies: the planned
economy in agriculture brought a huge increase in employment
in administrative organization, and the rise of many new small-
town institutions created a labor market for the peasants. Thus
the enlargement of institutions seeking untrained white-collar
workers, as well as the fear of collectivization and a reluctance
to work in collective farming, caused the increase in white-
collar peasant-workers. After 1956, when a great many productive cooperatives were disbanded and the peasants took back
their farms, they continued to hold their positions in the institutions where they had become thoroughly and firmly entrenched.
Although the movement of peasants to white-collar work did not
change the character of the intelligentsia in cities and small
towns, it nonetheless had a strong influence on the composition
and functions of the rural intelligentsia. The traditional authority of the priest, the teacher, and the druggist was displaced
by the local "power elite," composed of the chairman of the village council, the secretary of the party organization, the chairman of the cooperative, and their co-workers.

These aspects of social changes in Poland played an important role in national life. Peasants in factories, schools, institutions, villages, and towns dictated a grass-roots social rhythm
as well as peasant ways of thinking and acting. They could not,
of course, exert a decisive influence, since they had neither
their own system of ideas to impose nor any program for re-
organizing society. To put it simply, before peasant ways
changed under the influence of new environments, these environments were adapted to the peasants' own demands and to their
own established lifestyles.

Summarizing the discussion of changes in the class structure
during the second stage of industrialization, we first observe
basic changes in the structure of traditional classes, those
which existed before the war and which in the years immediately
after the war reconstructed themselves along the lines of previously established patterns. The groundwork for new principles
of social differentiation and for a new system of stratification
was also developed. During this period researchers' attention
was focused primarily on the changes in size, composition, and
function of the traditional classes within the total framework.
But during this stage a socialist state, with its attendant cen-
trally planned economic and government institutions, was being
created.

In this new social structure the importance of certain occupations increased greatly, particularly those which were especially necessary for industrialization and the building of the
system. The basic stratifying factor, however, was the domain
of political and economic decisions.

In a developing system political institutions are the dominant
institutions, and they subordinate all other types of institutions
and all fields of endeavor. Thus participation in political decisions implies influence in all other areas of public life. Grass-
roots interest and pressure groups emerge from these conditions.

The Complementary Stage

Changes in the class and stratum structure during the period
of complementary industrialization increasingly reflect changes
in the labor force. It is a period of progressive diminution of
the social significance of the old differentiation and stratification systems, a crystallization of new social differentiation
principles, and the growing importance of various interest groups.
These changes result primarily from the functioning of the political system and the principles of the exercise of political
power and from the functioning of the economic system and
principles of sharing the national income. The school system

and educational level must be relegated to a position of less importance in the formation of a new social hierarchy.

Two basic processes that changed the macrostructure of Polish society proceeded until 1970 along almost the same lines as those established toward the end of the fifties: the transformation of classes and traditional strata and the formation of new criteria for social differentiation.

In the middle of the sixties one could have gotten the impression that traditional classes were losing their significance. It seemed that the limitation of the market by the planned economy greatly reduced the conflict of economic interests among classes, that these interests were reconciled by the actions of the central planner, and that therefore the struggle of class interests was diminishing. It also seemed that class political interests had stopped playing a role in public life because the possibility of influencing political change was minimized. The old traditional classes, therefore, were not able to intervene in the development processes shaping the future of the society, and it was assumed that they would quietly fade into the past.

In the sixties, then, the process of working-class integration stimulated great interest among sociologists. Individuals who sought employment after 1945 were able to find work as manual laborers, and they had melted into the working class after twenty-five years. This was a different working class than the one whose ideological vision was nurtured by union and political activists. It was a class shaped by real work conditions and the functioning of socialist industry in its actual, nonideal form. Therefore the events of December 1970 astonished all those who stubbornly maintained that the actual development of society had been congruent with its ideologically inspired vision.

The rise in qualification levels and the stress on technical training and on the quality of work (especially in the second half of the sixties) were hampered by a system of wages and premiums that made the effort to raise qualifications unprofitable. However, changes in occupational composition were still taking place; and despite all the inhibiting factors, modernization continued, for it was inevitable.

The age structure of the working class was changing, "rejuvenating" that class. The system created much higher aspirations in younger generations of workers than it had in the peasants who began work in the fifties. In the sixties the working class was transforming itself into a class much more aware of its own interests.

At the same time, the potential existed in the working class for markedly accelerating the economic development of the country. The level of education and qualification was significantly higher than in the fifties, and there was a willingness to expend great effort through the instrument of a rational organization and a rational system of wages and premiums. This class was ripe for a great leap forward, a creative development of its potential, but it awaited a program and some organizational forms that might facilitate this. Through its direct intervention in 1970 it made both possible.

The development of the intelligentsia in the sixties will be described by future historians as the continued diminution of hopes awakened after 1956, as the continuation of professionalization processes, of attempts at directing development in accordance with modernization requirements, and at the same time, of settling into a stabilized system.

The previously outlined development trends from the period of basic industrialization were still operative. The influence of industrialization on the intelligentsia, however, was filtered through the sieve of the then existing forms of the political system. The number of workers with higher and secondary education was increasing, as was the scope of the communication media and, therefore, also the influence of the intelligentsia whom we have termed "verbal technicians."

No basic changes took place in the transformation of peasants. The process of creation of the peasant-farmers continued, although at a much slower rate, and the number of worker-peasants increased. The process of urbanization was unfolding in the country; increasing numbers of machines, television sets, motorcycles, chemicals, chemical fertilizers, and other items of technical progress were spread more widely. The processes of raising the educational level and of recruitment of young people into nonfarming occupations continued, although the attractiveness of farming was also increasing. State farms grew stronger and were becoming centers of agricultural progress, and those production cooperatives which had survived and achieved a substantial level of affluence were similarly progressing. Agricultural policy supported the establishment of specialized farms. Economic differentiation of the stratum of peasants who owned their farms became increasingly dependent on their specialized knowledge, organizational capabilities, and industriousness.

The stratification and division into the categories of peasant-farmers, farmer-workers, white-collar worker-peasants, and peasant private entrepreneurs persisted; but at the same time, there were indications that it would not last beyond one or two generations. The children of these "bistratum" individuals will more likely choose a life in the more attractive of the two environments, that is, city life.

In the sixties the basic factor that cut across all the traditional strata and classes in Polish society was stratification resulting from political and administrative power, income level, and the level of education. One could also enumerate other differentiating tendencies and the stratification resulting from them, but these three were the most important. The interesting thing about this new social differentiation was the fact that it created its own strata, which were social aggregates rather than internally cohesive class groupings. Those class-producing factors which operate in capitalist society (e.g., familial accumulation of wealth and power) did not appear in Poland. No political or economic policy encouraged the transmission of either wealth or power to the next generation. The differentiating influence of education was not associated with either income or political power. The sixties were also years of stability in this regard.

Notes

1. C. Kerr et al., Industrialism and Industrial Man (Cambridge, Mass., 1960).

2. Z. A. Karpiński, Zagadnienia socialistycznej industrializacji polski (Warsaw, 1958); B. Minc, O strukturze gospodarki Polski Ludowej (Warsaw, 1964); J. Pajestka, Kierunki doskonalenia systemu planowania i zarządzania w Polsce Ludowej (Warsaw, 1964); K. Secomski, Wstęp do teorii rozmieszczenia sit wytworczych (Warsaw, 1956).

3. J. Szczepański, "Zmiany w strukturze klasowej społeczeństwa polskiego," in A. Sarapata, ed., Przemiany społeczne w Polsce Ludowej (Warsaw, 1965).

Włodzimierz Wesołowski

THE INFLUENCE OF TECHNICAL-ECONOMIC AND HISTORICAL-CULTURAL CONTEXTS ON THE DIFFERENTIATION AND INTEGRATION OF SOCIAL CLASSES*

Research to Date and New Research Needs

Postwar Polish sociological literature contains many interesting studies describing changes in the fundamental components of our class structure: the working class, the peasantry (farmers), and the white-collar stratum, colloquially referred to as the intelligentsia.[1] Although the literature on class structure in Polish sociology is relatively extensive, it does not provide an integrated, many-sided description of the social classes and relations between them. Future research should prepare the material needed to create such a picture, and future theories must supply the assumptions and framework necessary to create a synthesis.

In the new research all the characteristics of social position in every class and, analogously, all the important intra- and interclass relations should be the object of a systematic analysis. One of the deficiencies of previous research on class structure in Poland as well as in other socialist countries is the fragmentary nature of the studies. Some researchers concern themselves with the working class, others with the intel-

*From Włodzimierz Wesołowski, Teoria, badania, praktyka: Z problematyki klasowej (Warsaw: Książka i Wiedza, 1975), pp. 283-99 and 304-11. Abridgements and minor editorial changes were introduced with the author's consent.

ligentsia, and still others with the peasantry. Some studies concentrate on job qualifications, others income, and still others cultural consumption or selected topics concerning public opinion. The results of these studies are generally not comparable because the research designs are dissimilar. In order to advance our knowledge, comparable studies should be conducted that cover the diverse phenomena characterizing class structure as well as the "inner life" of specific classes.

If the goal of empirical research is to obtain a rich image of the life of social classes and strata, we must become clearly aware of the scope of the phenomena that should be investigated. This is an attempt to enumerate and group them.

In the first group we should place the "class attributes" that appear in Marxism as the definitional criteria of social classes. They are the relationship to the means of production, the position occupied in the social organization of labor, and the form and degree of relative shares in the national income.

In the second group we can place the broadly understood material conditions of life, including patterns and levels of consumption of material goods, and the qualitative and quantitative aspects of participation in cultural life.

The third group of phenomena concerns class consciousness. This is, in particular, a question of the awareness of common interests in the various classes, feelings of class solidarity and class identification, attitudes toward socioeconomic systems, and perceptions of social history, including their own place in it.

The fourth group (closely related to the previous one) consists of different forms of sociopolitical activity that occur primarily in political parties, labor unions (especially among workers), cooperative organizations (especially among peasants), and professional associations (particularly among the intelligentsia).

Intraclass Differentiation

At different stages in the development of a socioeconomic

system (capitalist or socialist), the basic class attributes take
on different forms, and the relative importance of each attribute varies. In the present phase of building socialism in our
country, the differences in relationship to means of production
allow one to distinguish employees of the national economy,
members of work cooperatives, and small commodity producers
with private means of production, who are mainly individual
farmers.

During the course of economic development, each of the kinds
of "relationship to the means of production" acquires a new
meaning. In our situation one can observe this, for example,
in the case of agricultural producers. Their control of private
means of production is subject to an increasing extent to gov-
ernmental "steering," and their individual economic decisions
are dependent to an ever increasing degree on collective forms
of labor, which take the form of mutual aid and cooperation.

In Poland the class of small individual farmers is now differentiated from the working class and the intelligentsia not only
by a different relationship to the means of production but also
by a differing character of work and by a different mechanism
of sharing in the national income (earnings versus profit). The
working class and the intelligentsia stratum differ from each
other above all in the nature of work (whether it is predominantly manual or nonmanual) and in educational and lifestyle
correlates. To these correlative traits one must add the conditions of material life.

Technological progress and social policy gradually bring
about a reduction in the differences between the working class
and the intelligentsia. It is also true that in the long run, the
general trend toward the socialization of agriculture will result
in an increasing similarity between all the social classes in
their relationship to the means of production. Concurrently,
the technical modernization of agriculture will take place (even
now we are seeing the first signs), bringing together both the
working conditions and the living standards of agricultural and
industrial workers.

Besides the need for detailed research on the differences

between classes, more attention must also be directed to differences within classes. This problem is being discussed in all the socialist countries. If considering a larger number of class-status attributes implies a greater breadth of analysis, then the analysis of intraclass differences implies more depth of investigation. This has theoretical as well as practical significance.

In our Polish research we decided to satisfy the widely felt need for a more detailed description of social structure by introducing socio-occupational groups as units for analyzing the intraclass differentiation of the urban population. Various aspects of the division of labor form the background for the classification of occupations. "The nature of work," whether it is predominantly manual or nonmanual, the level of professional qualifications, and whether the work involves supervisory or submissive functions in the management process — all these are taken into account when dividing the employed population into socio-occupational groups.

Research on intraclass differentiation has both a general and a specific rationale. It is not difficult, for example, to note that changes leading to the lessening of global class differences do not happen uniformly in all segments of the class structure. Thus, for example, changes in the character of work and the standard of living affect certain sectors of the working class more than others. The advancement of workers with high qualifications in modern industry is much more rapid than the advancement of workers with low qualifications working in industry with stable technology. Analogous situations may be observed among the intelligentsia and the class of small farmers.

The introduction of intraclass divisions into the studies of global social structure is justified by such considerations as:

1) Technological and social policy changes have caused whole occupational groups to shift their positions, resulting in advancement or relative demotion.

2) Changes in the configuration of social status characteristics within socio-occupational groups have not proceeded uniformly.

40

Differentiation and Integration of Social Classes

3) Social mobility has brought about greater diversity in the social origins of the incumbents of various socio-occupational groups, with manifold consequences.

Technical-Economic and Historical-Cultural Contexts

Up to this point we have considered the need to study intra-class differences from a strictly descriptive point of view, but these studies could gain a deeper theoretical meaning by relating this description to hypotheses concerning social dynamics. I would like to draw attention to such a possibility through the discussion of two "contexts" in which structural changes take place. Here we are speaking of contexts that can be termed "technical-economic" and "historical-cultural."

The need for initiating comparative studies of the social structure of European socialist countries has been expressed with increasing frequency. The advantages of such studies include discovery of cross-national patterns in changes of class structure in socialist countries and, concurrently, the disclosure of specific national characteristics in the development of this structure. Not enough attention was paid to this problem in the early stages of empirical investigation.

Thus the concept of contexts would be one of the theoretical tools for studying the development of class structure in individual countries. Small contextual effects imply uniformity of developmental processes, whereas large contextual effects suggest evidence of diversifying processes. In replication studies designed to reveal the dynamics of change, one could analyze whether differentiating and unifying factors have constant effects over time or whether the strength of effects depends on the particular phase of development.

By technical-economic context we mean the conditioning of structural changes inherent in processes of technological development, in transformations of property relations, and in changes in management systems. Among these processes, without a doubt the most important is the phase of development

41

of the socialist state and its substages. In Poland this denotes, among other things, socioeconomic changes in agriculture, the industrialization process, and the rate and direction of technical and organizational changes brought about by the scientific-technical revolution. At the same time, I would like to give some idea of the scope of elements that should be considered if the concept of technical-economic context is to be used to explain concrete characteristics of the class structure in a given time period. If one wanted to operationalize the term "context," it would require a careful analysis and classification of the factors mentioned above.

Along with socioeconomic development the discussion of context should include a second general aspect of national economic management, the aspect which we shall call "organizational." Two socialist societies can be at the same stage and substage of general development, but their class-stratum structures can differ in certain respects as a result of a different direction of investment (they may have differing resource bases or may have undertaken different tasks in the international division of labor). Other reasons for differences in the class structures may be dissimilar forms of organizing production and planning units or varying wage systems and mechanisms of social policy.

These properties of the economic systems taken together (although not necessarily by themselves) form mechanisms "producing" specified sets of social status characteristics of specific occupational groups. Among the European socialist countries there exists a strong unifying tendency that leads to similar solutions in planning and management and in the realm of social and economic policy. But this tendency does not eliminate the diversity of detailed solutions that should be considered when studying class structure.

One might suppose that diversities resulting from the "organizational" aspect are more tangible at the level of socioeconomic groups than for whole classes. When we take into account different stages of development, the diversities resulting from them will become clear even at the level of classes (e.g., the size of the working class, its division among industries,

Differentiation and Integration of Social Classes

differences in educational level).

The historical-cultural context encompasses group patterns of behavior, aspirations, and value systems rooted not in the current technical-economic system but in past experience and social relations. Marx frequently drew attention to the fact that the cultural past encumbers the present, especially through attitudes, aspirations, and preferences. Taking into account Marx's remarks, research on structural changes would require the elaboration of problems pertaining to the persistence from the past of some elements in class psychology, or even in institutional arrangements, through the impact of tradition and socialization. Today's patterns of behavior do not emerge spontaneously or naturally out of present conditions. There are powerful forces of continuity and inertia.

Many studies on the social structure of socialist countries assume that in urban populations employed in the national economy, the character of work determines the level of wages, the cultural level, and many other attributes of social standing. Such statements, if properly constructed, are equivalent to statistical laws. We have decided to determine empirically to which aspects of work they apply. One can also ask whether these statistical relations are equally strong in all socio-occupational classes and categories.

We have proposed a hypothesis on the influence of a specific historical-cultural context on the discrepancies connecting three variables: skills required for work, income, and cultural consumption. Our book Social Differentiation provides appropriate data that address this hypothesis.[2] We found that the intelligentsia stratum was first divided into groups with higher and lower qualifications. The group having lower qualifications has been further divided into two subgroups: technicians and office workers. In this way we have obtained subgroups with similar qualifications but with different types of education and work. We found that technicians received higher pay than office workers, but their cultural consumption was more or less the same. These differences show that in terms of remuneration, work in technical occupations is given a higher social evalua-

43

tion; but cultural level is shaped independently of wage level. We surmise that in Poland this differentiation occurs because there is a strong tendency among office workers to imitate the lifestyle of the intelligentsia. Perhaps the same effect occurs in other socialist countries. If it does not, this would be a historical-cultural effect.

Intraclass and Interclass Integration

The problematics of class relations are extremely important in considering social classes. Unfortunately, and this criticism applies to myself as well as to Polish sociology in general, they have been inadequately studied. Neglect is especially apparent in empirical research.

Let us begin by recalling that social structure has three main aspects: first, a set of characteristics distinguishing classes; second, a set of relations between classes; third, a set of relations characterizing the internal cohesion of classes. In Marx's theory these three sets form an interrelated complex. Complete and exhaustive studies of class structure should include all three aspects. Likewise, studies on the transformation of class structure and on its present shape in our society should also include them.

Even a cursory knowledge of sociological literature suggests that until now empirical studies on the class-stratum structure have concentrated on sets of characteristics. The problems of interclass and intraclass relations have remained in the background. Some studies of the Polish United Workers' Party and worker self-government have touched on this topic, but they have not treated it as an integral part of studies on class structure. Hence the analysis of intraclass and interclass relations is currently a very important issue.

Neglect of this area is not accidental. Let us begin with the simplest causes. In sociology as a whole the methodology for studying class relations is less developed than the methodology for studying correlations among individual characteristics.

Differentiation and Integration of Social Classes

Moreover, the investigation of class relations must be combined with theoretical considerations in a particularly conscious and thoughtful way. The operationalization of theoretical concepts is more difficult in this area than it is for social status characteristics. None of this, however, should excuse us from efforts to engage in research on class relations.

It is only necessary to recall that in Marx's theory there exists a complex of various kinds of relations between classes. A similar complex, though probably having fewer components, integrates the social class or stratum internally. In order to illustrate the complexity and variety involved, I will refer to the classic example: relations between the bourgeoisie and the proletariat under capitalism. These classes are characterized by antagonistic relations of economic exploitation and political domination that assume different intensity and forms at different stages of capitalism. The actors in this conflict can be individuals, groups of workers, and unorganized crowds, as well as labor unions and political parties. Alienation is manifested both in everyday life and in strike conflicts, and concurrently, intraclass solidarity develops.

What are the interclass and intraclass relations in a socialist system? We can say that we know their basic forms. We know, for example, which of those existing in capitalism have been eliminated, which have undergone essential transformations or even "reversal" (e.g., class hegemony). Their real shape, however, the daily means of their formation and common modes of functioning have not yet become the subject of penetrating analysis.

My primary purpose is to advocate an intensification of theoretical and empirical studies on three kinds of relations: relations of solidarity and internal integration of the working class; economic and psychological relations between the working class, farmers, and intelligentsia; interclass integration in the form of national integration of the socialist society.

Intraclass integration is important because it has the potential for overcoming the internal differentiation of the working class evidenced by inequalities among its socio-occupational groups. Objective and subjective common interests, solidarity in group political action, or a strong self-identification with the class and its economic goals are the factors that serve to integrate class members despite occupational differentiation, unequal incomes and education, and differing world views.

One cannot even begin to consider the processes of integration within the Polish working class without referring to the history of this class in recent decades, particularly during wartime, liberation, and rapid industrialization. Many writers have paid attention to such facts as the dispersal of the working class during the German occupation, the transfer of the most productive workers to the reconstruction of the economy and government, and the influx of nonproletarian elements at the time of initial extensive industrialization during the six-year plan. In this first postwar period, the problems of integration of the working class consisted of professional training, adaptation to the discipline of work and the principles of cooperation, and attempts at reducing conflicts between different social and regional groups. Some of these phenomena were studied to some extent by sociologists. Today the problems of working-class integration are qualitatively different, and we should direct our attention to them. The basic issue seems to be the process of increasing political integration and rising political aspirations.

Processes of political integration include actions and attitudes for which the frame of reference is the interest of classes as a whole and issues of the country at large. Organizations through which this integration proceeds are primarily party organizations and, additionally, union organizations and worker self-government. For this reason research on these three kinds of organizations and their activities, the determination of factors that increase and strengthen their role in the factory and in specific groups of the work-team, is an extremely important element in the whole area of research on intraclass cohesion.

In the field of interclass relations, I would like to stress only one problem, but one closely concerned with the problem of self-government and internal integration of the working class. It is the question of the role of this class in the political life of the country, and thus also its role in relation to other classes and strata. This is, to use classical terminology, the problem of working-class hegemony. We have resolved this problem with generalities much too frequently. Such generalities should not become a substitute for more thorough studies.

The political and ideological hegemony of any class has several dimensions. The fundamental dimension is undoubtedly the leadership of the party of this class in political life and its ideological dominance in the society. But other dimensions of hegemony do exist. Here I would include: the immediate involvement of rank-and-file members of the class in politics; the cultural influence of the class; and the place in the society's system of values of the activities represented by the average member of the class.

The political hegemony of the working class and leadership of its party implies, above all, leadership among its class and party allies. The internal solidarity of the working class in a socialist system does not lead to antagonistic relations with other classes and strata. It is a solidarity that has possibilities for generalization to the entire nation. Although it is premature to consider transformations that will occur in the distant future, we can now pose the question: What role will be played in society as a whole by the organizational framework that already exists among the working class? I have in mind, for example, the extension of worker self-government. The question seems justified since there are already the beginnings of farmer self-government. Will the employees of nonindustrial enterprises also become integrated through self-government? What common features of the functioning of all types of self-governments and which political programs will generate and strengthen national solidarity?

Notes

1. Editors' note: The author refers to a series of empirical studies conducted in Poland between 1956 and 1970.
2. W. Wesołowski, ed., Zróżnicowanie społeczne (Wrocław: Ossolineum, 1970).

47

Krzysztof Zagórski

URBANIZATION AND RESULTING CHANGES IN CLASS STRUCTURE AND EDUCATION*

The Urbanization Process and Labor Force Composition

The process of urbanization in Poland is characterized by a more rapid increase in nonfarm population than in urban population. In the twenty-year period 1950-70, the population in the cities rose from 9.6 to 17 million, while the population in rural areas rose only from 15 to 15.6 million. Thus almost the entire population increase in Poland took place in the cities despite the fact that the rate of natural population increase is higher in the country than in the cities. In the same twenty-year period, however, the number of people earning a living outside farming grew from 13 to 23 million, and the farming population decreased from around 12 to 9.6 million.

The much more rapid increase in rural nonfarm population than in urban population arises chiefly from an inadequate rate of development of urban construction that impedes migration from country to city. Moreover, the modernization of farming and the general sociocultural development of the country have

*From Krzysztof Zagórski, "Robotnicy w strukturze społeczno-zawodowej," in Jan Szczepański, Narodziny socjalistycznej klasy robotniczej (Warsaw: Instytut Wydawniczy Centralnej Rady Związków Zawodowych, 1974), pp. 197-206 and 220-26. Abridgements and small editorial changes were introduced by the editors with the author's consent.

resulted in the rapid growth of occupational groups not directly engaged in agricultural production but related to it. Among the most important sectors that perform various agriculture-related services are trade, transport and communication, education and health services, employing workers as well as industrial and service sector administrators and local government officials. In effect, the percentage of the rural population earning a living from nonfarm sources has grow very large and in 1970 amounted to 42.9%. A number of persons whose main income is derived from nonagricultural sources but who draw additional income from agriculture are included in this group.

Table 1

Urban and Nonfarm Population, 1921-70*

	Urban Population		Nonfarm Population		
Year	percent of total population	percent of labor force	percent of total population	percent of labor force	percent of labor force employed in industry
1921	24.6	18.1	34.0	22.6	8.7
1931	27.4	21.9	40.0	29.7	12.0
1950	39.0	33.2	52.9	43.4	18.8
1960	48.3	41.8	61.6	52.9	23.3
1970	52.2	48.4	70.5	63.5	27.6

*Source: Data of the General National Census.

Transformations of the Socio-occupational Structure

Transformations of the socio-occupational structure which occurred in Poland after the Second World War were at first concerned chiefly with changes in the social system and later with promoting rapid economic growth.

The group of large landowners suffered dissolution as a result of the first of these two factors, and the number of petite bourgeoisie and individual craftsmen was reduced to a minimum. Land reforms also led to a decrease in the size of the agrarian proletariat, giving land to landless peasants who had previously earned a living by working as rural hired laborers. This category comprised over one third of all manual laborers before the war, but it now numbers less than one tenth.

Changes in the system as well as rapid socioeconomic development have caused a considerable increase in the size of the working class. The general rise in the number of workers and their increase as a proportion of the labor force came about despite the decline in the rural proletariat mentioned above; hence this rise was related to the increase in nonagricultural employment.

The continuing demand for education, the increasing complexity of the management process, and the development of the service sectors of the economy caused a much more rapid increase in white-collar workers than in manual workers.

The growth in manual workers, however, was also characterized by a great explosion. In 1970 more than 6.6 million manual workers were employed in the national economy, compared with 4.7 million in 1960. If we add to manual workers the number of agricultural-cooperative and other types of cooperative workers who perform physical tasks, the size of this group exceeds 6.8 million people. Manual workers constitute the largest group in the socio-occupational structure. In 1970 they made up about 40% of the total labor force, and their proportion has been systematically increasing since the twenty-year period between the world wars.

The growth in the working class was accomplished mostly through assimilation of peasants, and it occurred in tandem with the rapid transformation of the economy. We have mentioned that the presence of large numbers of manual workers in the occupational structure does not in itself tell us very much about the most important aspects of this structure. A pertinent issue here is the distribution of manual workers among the various sectors of the national economy.

After rapid structural transformations in the course of the first fifteen-year period after the war, we see no significant changes in the labor-force distribution of manual workers

Urbanization and Class Structure

among economic sectors despite the considerable increase in
their number. It may be surmised that this is related to reaching a phase of socioeconomic growth in which there is a reduction in the rate of increase of industrial and construction workers as a proportion of the labor force. More recently labor-
force composition has exhibited a shift of workers out of the
production sector and into the service sector. The increased
number of workers employed in industry (working in a setting

Table 2

Composition of the Labor Force
by Socio-occupational Groups, 1921-70 (in %)

Socio-occupational groups	1921	1931	1950	1960	1970‡
Total	100	100	100	100	100
Workers	26.0	29.4	43.9	51.7	61.3
blue-collar	22.7	25.3	—	33.5	39.3
white-collar	3.3	4.1	—	18.2	22.0
Members of work cooperatives	—	—	1.3	2.3	2.3
Members of agricultural production cooperatives	—	—	0.4	0.2	0.2
Individual farmers*	66.0	60.7	52.6	44.0	33.7
Self-employed, non-agricultural†	6.7	9.5	1.6	1.5	1.3
Other	0.6	0.4	0.2	0.3	1.2

Source: Data of the General National Census, with additional calculations made by the author.
*Those working as self-employed in agriculture, including those
family members helping them.
†Including those family members helping the self-employed outside
agriculture.
‡The classification of occupational groups applied to the results of
the 1970 General National Census differed somewhat from that applied
to previous censuses. To preserve comparability the data in this table
are presented after appropriate adjustments. Because of this they may
differ somewhat from data taken from official census publications, in
which members of work-cooperatives and agricultural production cooperatives are included with the workers.

51

Krzysztof Zagórski

of formal employment relations) during this phase results more from the rise in employment of the technical and managerial work force than from a rise in the employment of blue-collar workers.

Manual workers in industry and construction, the group closest to the stereotype of the working class, includes less than two thirds of all manual workers. This group contains 4.2 million workers. About 15%, or 1.0 million manual workers, are employed in transport, communications, and trade. These areas of manual labor are marginally included in the working class since the jobs share some characteristics of white-collar occupations.

It is true that the relative share employed in industry and construction has stayed approximately the same during the last ten years. The change is enormous, however, in relation to the period before the war. The proportion of construction workers has increased over five times since the early nineteen thirties, and that of workers employed in industry has almost doubled.

As noted above, the prominent group in the socio-occupational structure of Poland before September 1939 was farm laborers, both on landed estates and on the larger farms. The large-scale use of hired labor in agriculture was related to the size of the landless rural population and its difficulty in finding nonagricultural employment. The number of agricultural laborers decreased drastically upon the implementation of land reform and the inception of socialist industrialization. Nonetheless, this group still occupies a vital position in the occupational structure, and over the last ten-year period it has increased slightly as a proportion of manual workers. This is true even though the share of the rural population has been decreasing. In 1970 there were a half-million agricultural laborers (not including members of agricultural production cooperatives).

The employment of a manual worker in a specific sector of the economy does not uniquely determine the nature of his work. A repairman fixing appliances can be employed by a university; an agricultural worker can be employed in industry, perhaps as a gardener, caring for the plant's grounds; a waitress can

52

Urbanization and Class Structure

Table 3

Distribution of Manual Workers
among Sectors of the Economy (in %)

Sectors	1921	1931	1960	1970*
Total	100	100	100	100
Nonagricultural	51.4	62.7	93.0	92.5
industry	21.5	27.4	50.0	51.5
construction	1.7	1.9	12.0	11.8
transport and communication	5.2	5.4	9.5	9.8
trade	2.1	3.0	6.5	5.4
education, research, and culture	0.3	0.6	2.6	3.3
health care, welfare, and				
recreation	0.4	1.3	3.0	3.0
other	20.2	23.1	8.6	7.7
Agricultural	48.6	37.3	7.0	7.5

Source: Data of the General National Census, with additional calculations made by the author.
*To insure comparability the data for 1970 exclude members of work-cooperatives and agricultural production cooperatives (in census publications these groups are included with workers).

work in a plant's cafeteria or diner; a driver might be employed in agriculture; a mason might work on a maintenance crew; and a mechanic can service agricultural machinery. For this reason the analysis of manual workers by economic sector is not sufficient. We must look beyond these aggregate divisions and determine the actual occupations in which these workers are employed and their place in the social division of labor. An analysis of socio-occupational groups will serve this purpose.

The socio-occupational structure of the population will be characterized using data only for that part of the labor force for whom work is their main source of income (excluding those for whom work constitutes a supplemental income). This group is referred to as the working population in official government publications, and we know somewhat more about it than about the entire labor force. This large category numbered 16.4 million in Poland in 1970.

53

Krzysztof Zagórski

In the last ten-year period there has been an increase in the relative share of the intelligentsia as well as a significant rise in the relative share of industrial, construction, and related workers in the socio-occupational structure. The increase in this last group is smaller than would appear from comparing the corresponding percentages in the tables because we should take into account that it was not possible to determine accu-

Table 4

Socio-occupational Composition of the Working Population*
in 1960 and 1970 (in %)

Socio-occupational Groups	1960	1970
Total	100	100
Workers and employees[†]	53.2	64.4
in administrative-management and office jobs	6.6	8.6
specialists in technical occupations[‡]	3.0	4.5
specialists in nontechnical occupations	3.3	4.6
workers in industrial, construction, and related occupations	14.5	25.3
laborers in various unskilled jobs	1.4	2.2
workers in transport, communication, trade, and nonindustrial service centers	5.7	10.4
unskilled service personnel	2.7	2.8
agricultural and forestry workers	1.9	2.3
workers in undetermined occupations	14.1	3.7
Farmers with additional employment	1.2	1.3
Members of agricultural production cooperatives	0.2	0.2
Individual farmers[§]	44.0	32.9
Others	1.4	1.2

Source: Data of the General National Census, with additional calculations made by the author.

*Not including individuals whose main source of income is derived from sources other than earnings.

[†]Including members of work-cooperatives.

[‡]Including forestry and agricultural engineers and members of related occupations.

[§]Including those with specialized farms (e.g., orchards, livestock, etc.).

54

rately the occupation of many manual workers in 1960, whereas in 1970 there were few individuals with undetermined occupations.

It can be assumed that the percentage of workers engaged in industrial construction and related work has increased from somewhat over 20% to over 25% of the total working population during the last ten years. We should also stress the expansion of transport, communication, trade, and nonindustrial service occupations. The rising importance of this socio-occupational group is a result of increased emphasis on industrial and personal services. Even now, the supply of these workers is not adequate in Poland, and we can expect a considerable acceleration of the rate of increase in the next few years.

Educational Levels

The level of education in Poland rose quite rapidly during the postwar years; nonetheless it is not yet considered high enough. Only one third of the total working population has more than an elementary education.

Among the three largest socio-occupational groups (manual workers, white-collar workers, and individual farmers), the white-collar workers naturally have the highest educational level. Over 80% of the workers in this group have more than an elementary education, compared to less than one third of manual workers and less than one twentieth of individual farmers.

The educational level of industrial, construction, and related workers compares favorably with other socio-occupational groups. One third of this group has basic vocational training, in principle assuring it a high level of worker qualification. Moreover, almost 5% can claim matriculation certificates, and a large majority have vocational certification.

The educational level of manual workers in transport, communication, trade, and nonindustrial service occupations is not as high. Only about 20% of these groups have more than an elementary education (seven years of schooling). On the other hand, better formal qualifications characterize white-collar

Table 5

Working Population* by Selected Socio-occupational Groups
and Educational Level, 1970 (in %)

Socio-occupational groups	Total	Educational level					
		higher	secondary		basic trade§	elementary‖	incomplete elementary#
			trade†	academic‡			
Total	100	3.6	10.3	4.8	15.0	42.4	23.9
Manual workers	100	0.1	3.2	1.0	25.2	56.0	14.5
workers in industrial, construction, and related occupations	100	0.0	3.8	0.9	32.8	52.0	10.5
laborers in various unskilled jobs	100	0.0	0.8	0.7	7.3	63.1	28.1
workers in transport and communication	100	0.0	1.8	0.8	19.4	72.2	5.3
workers in trade, storage, and nonindustrial services	100	0.0	2.5	1.7	20.2	57.8	17.8
unskilled service personnel	100	0.0	0.7	0.7	4.8	63.0	30.8
agriculture and forestry workers	100	0.1	0.9	0.3	5.9	58.3	34.5
White-collar workers	100	15.4	37.2	17.8	12.6	16.5	0.5
workers in transport and communication	100	1.3	22.1	19.6	21.2	35.3	0.5
workers in trade, storage, and nonindustrial services	100	1.1	13.2	8.1	32.7	44.2	0.7
Individual farmers	100	0.0	0.7	0.4	3.6	42.3	53.0

Source: Data of the General National Census.
*Not including those who have a nonwage main source of income. †Including postsecondary. ‡Including incomplete higher education. §Including incomplete trade secondary. ‖Including incomplete academic secondary and incomplete basic trade. #Including no formal education.

workers employed in similar occupations.

Laborers employed in various unskilled jobs, unskilled service personnel, and agricultural and forestry workers differ considerably from the remaining socio-occupational groups in level of education. They are the least educated of all groups.

Dual Occupations

In 1970, 1.2 million persons in the labor force had more than one job. This group constituted 7.5% of the total working population. The principal occupation of these individuals was on a self-owned or individual family farm; the other was off the farm.

The existence of this group is related to the specific nature of socioeconomic development in our country, and it constitutes one of the main urbanizing influences on the Polish countryside. It favors the diffusion of the working-class lifestyle to rural society, although one can also speak of a certain "rustification" of the working class. This is caused both by the appreciable number of dual job-holders in it who are directly associated with the countryside and by the increase in the number of workers of peasant origin.

The dual-occupational population, working simultaneously in individual farming and outside it, is usually termed "worker-peasant." Nonetheless there are a number of categories within this group that make it difficult to call everyone in it "worker-peasants."

Among those working both on their own farms and in an additional job, nearly 75% were persons employed as manual workers; 25% of the group in question was composed of persons employed off their farms in white-collar work or other socio-occupational groups.

Occupations in trade, transport, communication, and nonindustrial services are relatively well represented in this population. One should also stress that about 10% of the workers having jobs outside their farms are administrative office workers or are in occupations classified as specialized. Thus the

data allow us to speak not only of "worker-peasants" but also
of "white-collar peasants."

We have discussed "worker-peasants" not only as an urbanizing influence in the countryside but also as a "ruralizing"
factor among the working class. It should also be noted that
more than one worker in ten who is engaged in industry, construction, and related occupations is quite directly involved in
agriculture by virtue of additional employment on his own farm.
This effect is even greater for certain other groups of manual
workers. Simultaneous employment in farming and outside of
it (most often in industry) is still a large-scale phenomenon in
Poland. A series of economic, social, and cultural problems
have resulted from it. As examples we might mention the need
to commute to work places, changes in task distribution in the
rural family and some weakening of its internal bonds, and the
somewhat worsened management of farmland. Other changes
are a greater flexibility of the work force, lessened work discipline outside of farming, increased monetary income in the
countryside, and closer contact with urban culture (quite often,
we might add, not with the best of that culture). All these phenomena are connected with processes of rapid industrialization,
and they can be treated as symptoms of an intermediate phase
in the socio-occupational transformation of the rural populace.

PART TWO
Social Mobility

Krzysztof Zagórski

TRANSFORMATIONS OF SOCIAL STRUCTURE AND SOCIAL MOBILITY IN POLAND*

Structural Changes and Social Mobility

Socioeconomic development is associated with dynamic changes in the utilization of the work force and, consequently, with rapid changes in the socio-occupational structure. In Poland, as in other socialist countries, these changes have resulted not only from a transformation of the economy but also from a new political system.

Large-scale flows between socio-occupational groups appear in all societies that are characterized by rapid economic growth. In socialist societies, however, changes are also caused by the implementation of a social policy that aims at equalizing opportunities for people from diverse social backgrouns and at eradicating barriers that divide the society.

The implementation of these goals proceeded in various ways in Poland. Depending on the concrete social-political circumstances, it ranged from a universal policy of assuring mass "social advancement" in the early phases of political change-over to the application of specific preferential measures in educational policy, especially in recruitment to colleges and sec-

*From Krzysztof Zagórski, "Zmiany w strukturze i ruchliwości społecznej w Polsce," Wiadomości Statystyczne 5 (1974), pp. 1-6. Abridgements and minor editorial changes have been made by the editors with the author's permission.

ondary schools. The development of adult education programs
and correspondence courses took on importance in the later
phase and continues to predominate among the measures intended to assure the decline of intergroup barriers in Polish
society.

One should study changes in the socio-occupational structure
from both the economic point of view, focusing on the evolution
of the economic and employment structures, and from the sociological viewpoint, taking into account aspects of social divisions, social advancement, and changes in social context.

Changes in the membership of socio-occupational groups
which are associated with changes in the social structure are
termed social mobility. The total amount of mobility is the
sum of intergenerational mobility (starting employment in a
group different from one's social background as determined
by parents' position) and intragenerational mobility (changing
one's socio-occupational position in the course of one's career).

Social mobility is very often associated with attainment of a
higher level of education, and it is also frequently related to
migration (for instance, from country to city). The most complete data on changes in the socio-occupational structure are
provided by census records. One cannot determine the magnitude of social mobility in modern societies on this basis, however, for it is generally higher than would be expected solely
from changes in the size of various groups.

Until the present time there has been a lack of systematic
research in Poland that would permit a measurement of social
mobility on a nationwide scale. This problem was examined
either in relation to specific groups (most often during the
course of other studies) or on the basis of nonrepresentative
samples. The first truly representative nationwide study of
socioeconomic mobility in Poland was performed in December
of 1972 by the Central Statistical Office. The study was designed by the former Statistical-Sociological Research Group
and conducted under the auspices of the Census Bureau, where
the initial phases of data processing were also performed.

Changes in Social Structure and Mobility

Choice of Sample, Scope, and
Method of Investigation

The study concerned the entire labor force, with the exception of members of so-called "collective dwellings," such as workers' hotels, dormitories, etc. Individuals between the ages of 15 and 69 were included in the analysis.

The random sample comprised 0.5% of the total population. A two-stage stratified random sample was used. In the first stage census areas were randomly selected. The areas constituting the so-called "basic sample of census areas" (making up 10% of all areas) were initially divided into urban and rural and then divided according to the number of dwellings (39 or fewer, 40 to 99, 100 to 149, and 150 or more). In each of the eight subgroups obtained in this fashion, the census areas were arranged according to regions (voivodships) and counties (poviats). Finally, the following were selected by systematic sampling:

5% of the areas containing up to 39 dwellings;
10% of the areas containing 40 to 99 dwellings;
15% of the areas containing 100 to 149 dwellings;
20% of the areas containing 150 or more dwellings.

Since the basic sample contained 10% of all census areas, the areas chosen from particular groups were 10% of the corresponding total number of such areas.

An updated listing of dwellings was made for each of the selected areas, eliminating in the process exceptional areas such as army barracks, other restricted compounds, or areas consisting solely of "collective dwellings." If both home dwellings and "collective dwelling" buildings were found within the same area, the area stayed in the sample, but the study was conducted only on the home dwellings.

The second stage of sample selection was the choice of dwellings. Systematic choice was also used in this case. Each dwelling in the sample areas with 39 or fewer dwellings was included in the study. Every other dwelling was chosen in the group of areas containing 40 to 99 dwellings; every third in the group containing 100 to 149 dwellings; and finally, in the group of the largest census areas every fourth dwelling was selected. Thus in each size group of census areas, both in the voivodship cross-section and the division of town and country, 5.0% of the dwellings constituting the "basic sample," or 0.5% of the total of all dwellings were chosen. It was assumed that 0.5% of the Polish labor force resided in these dwellings, and the study encompassed all persons in the labor force living in the dwellings chosen. After excluding the population inhabiting "restricted areas" and "collective dwellings," 72,179 working people in the 15-69 age bracket were studied.

According to estimates this comprises about 91% of the total sample. A precise determination of the number of persons who should be included in the study is not possible owing to a lack of accurate data on the total population. This absence of an accurate estimate arises from the fact that the survey was made two years after the General Census and because of differences in the definition of the labor force applied in the Census and the survey.

In the 1970 General Census persons on active military duty, as well as those in penal institutions, if previously employed, were included in the labor force. Since it was impossible to use such a definition in the study of socio-occupational mobility, both of the above categories were omitted as currently not employed.

About 9% of the selected subjects were not studied owing to difficulties of the interviewers in finding them at home, travel, illness, refusal to answer questions (participation in the study could not be made compulsory), and other such causes.

Comparison of the socio-occupational structure among persons included in this study with the structure obtained as a result of the 1970 General Census shows a high degree of agreement between these sources, even in the case of the smallest categories. This leads us to surmise that the omission of 9% of the sample referred to above did not produce any systematic error and did not distort the results (see Table 3, pp. 74-75).

The study was carried out by specially trained interviewers who visited the dwellings selected and completed the questionnaires on the basis of personally conducted interviews.

The purpose of the study was to obtain accurate information on socio-occupational position, education, and place of residence of the respondents at two points in time: at the time of their first employment, and at the time of the study. Moreover, information was collected on the social background of the respondents, i.e., on the socio-occupational position and education of their parents at the time when the respondents began work. A variety of additional pertinent information was gathered: items such as place and year of birth, year of initial employment, year education was completed, manner of acquiring individual farms, marital status, and number and socio-occupational position of working siblings.

The study analyzed the relationship of various characteristics both for single respondents and for married couples. The primary characteristic studied was socio-occupational status. Accurate records of information about work performed, positions held, and socioeconomic groups made it possible for us to use three different classification schemes. Results are presented in terms of each scheme, and each differs in degree of detail.

A. Socioeconomic groups. This is the breakdown traditionally used in statistical records and the General Census, a classification into groups usually termed "social categories" in official statistics (blue-collar workers, white-collar workers, self-employed in and outside agriculture, and the remaining smaller groups, such as contract workers and artisans). Since the term "social category" is used in sociological studies to mean something totally different than in official statistics, we used the term "socioeconomic groups," which is also sometimes applied.

Although many investigators stress the diminishing social significance and the many drawbacks of this classification, we nonetheless used it in this study, mainly to relate our results to earlier statistical data. In any event, it has not totally lost its usefulness.

B. Socio-occupational groups. The classification of socio-occupational groups (containing over twenty categories) com-

bines information on socioeconomic grouping with data on the
specific character of the work performed, e.g., specialists in
technical areas, administrative management and office workers,
laborers in industrial and related jobs, workers in fields related to trade and nonindustrial services, etc.

C. Occupational groups. This is an additional classification
into specific vocations, used for more precise characterization
of certain socio-occupational groups. The sample size does
not permit an analysis of results using the full classification of
occupational groups, and for this reason only relatively large
vocational groups, such as physicians, teachers, miners, etc.,
were singled out.

Using this classification scheme enabled us not only to determine general trends in social mobility but also to study the occurrence of "inherited occupations," often associated with family vocational traditions.

The initial basic results of the study are presented below in
abridged form.

Changes in Socio-occupational Structure

The dynamic nature of change in the structure of Polish society is best evidenced by the fact that the proportion of manual
workers in the labor force has increased from about one quarter in 1931 to about one third in 1960, and finally to about 40%
in the first years of the 1970s.

In the same time period the proportion of white-collar workers in the social structure has increased more than fivefold
and has stabilized at nearly one fourth of the total labor force.
On the other hand, the proportion of individual farm owners
decreased by one half. Such pronounced changes in the socio-
occupational structure must have produced large increases in
social mobility processes, both inter- and intragenerational.
This effect is expressed in the social origins of the various
socioeconomic groups.

66

Changes in Social Structure and Mobility

Table 1

Labor Force Classified by Socioeconomic Groups,
1931-72 (in %)

Socioeconomic groups	1931	1960	1972
Total	100.0	100.0	100.0
Workers*	29.7	52.0	65.5
blue-collar*	25.6	33.8	42.2
white-collar*	4.1	18.2	23.3
Members of work-cooperatives	—	1.3	—
Members of agricultural pro- duction cooperatives	—	0.2	—
Self-employed outside agri- culture†	9.5	1.5	1.2
Self-employed in agriculture†	60.7	44.0	32.5
Other	0.1	0.0	0.9

Sources: 1931 and 1960, Census data; 1972, data from representative study of social mobility.

*In 1972 members of work-cooperatives and agricultural production cooperatives are included.

†Including those assisting the self-employed.

Social Mobility between Socioeconomic Groups

The socioeconomic position of parents at the time of a respondent's first job was taken as the point of departure in the analysis of social mobility. This stems from our conviction that more than anything else, the type and amount of education received as well as initial occupation are affected by social origin. The subsequent course of the occupational career is dependent to a much higher degree (although not entirely) on the personal attributes and predispositions of the individual. The current social position of the respondents results from the combined effects of both these factors.

In analyzing the social origins of a particular group, we will focus our attention predominantly on the father's social position, since in large measure it determines the social position of the entire family. The most homogeneous group in terms of social origin is owners of individual farms. Influx to this group from other social backgrounds is slight; nearly 90% of the farmers have fathers also cultivating farms of their own. While individual farm owners form a highly homogeneous group, at the same time they constitute an aggregate characterized by a large outflow to other socioeconomic groups. Among the labor force of rural background, almost a third work as blue-collar workers, and only 55% have remained in their fathers' socioeconomic group, that is, working on their own farms. Because of this, persons of rural background make up almost 40% of the blue-collar workers and over 25% of the white-collar workers.

Table 2

Socioeconomic Groups in 1972 and
Socioeconomic Groups of Fathers (in %)

Socioeconomic groups of fathers	Total*	Blue-collar workers	White-collar workers	Self-employed outside agriculture	Individual farmers
Total [†]	100.0	100.0	100.0	100.0	100.0
Blue-collar workers	32.9	48.0	38.8	28.9	9.0
White-collar workers	9.0	5.8	26.3	7.7	0.7
Self-employed outside agriculture	2.7	2.7	3.9	17.3	1.2
Individual farmers	51.7	38.4	26.8	41.8	87.6
Total [‡]	100.0	42.2	23.3	1.2	32.5
Blue-collar workers	100.0	61.5	27.5	1.0	8.9
White-collar workers	100.0	27.3	68.3	1.0	2.4
Self-employed outside agriculture	100.0	41.9	34.4	7.6	14.7
Individual farmers	100.0	31.3	12.1	1.0	55.0

*The category "others" is omitted.

[†]Social origins of 1972 employed by socioeconomic groups of fathers.

[‡]Socioeconomic groups of children (1972) by socioeconomic groups of fathers.

Changes in Social Structure and Mobility

The second most homogeneous socioeconomic group in terms of origins is the blue-collar workers. Almost half of them have fathers also engaged in manual labor. Among blue-collar workers characterized by a different social origin, individuals of rural background are dominant. Only 5% come from white-collar families. This relatively low percentage will, however, acquire an entirely different significance if we realize that of all persons whose fathers were white-collar workers, over one fourth work in blue-collar jobs. Thus social mobility from the white-collar to the blue-collar group can be regarded as fairly high in terms of outflow, and the relatively small effect of this mobility on the composition of the blue-collar group arises from the considerable difference in the size of these groups.

The share of white-collar workers among persons of blue-collar origin is almost identical to the share of blue-collar workers among those whose fathers worked in white-collar jobs, that is, slightly higher than one fourth. However, since the blue-collar group is much larger than that of white-collar workers among both the respondents and their fathers, the percentage of individuals of blue-collar background in the white-collar group is very high (nearly 40%).

Only one fourth of the white-collar workers had fathers belonging to the same socioeconomic group. This is about equal to the percent of white-collar workers coming from farm families. Thus nearly three fourths of the white-collar workers are recruited from other social milieux.

The self-employed outside agriculture are distinguished by even more diverse social backgrounds. Moreover, people coming from this group will in the overwhelming majority assume work outside it. To a large extent this probably arises from the marginal status of this particular group (only 1.2% of the total labor force) in our society and from its association with the relatively weak position of the private sector outside agriculture.

The individual's social position is affected by the social position of both his father and mother, with the two factors having a clearly additive effect. For example, 61.5% of all persons whose fathers did manual work are in the blue-collar group, but this figure is 66.0% among those whose parents were both manual workers and only 41.3% among the subgroup in which the fathers worked manually and the mothers did white-collar work.

Of all respondents whose fathers were white-collar workers, 68.3% are employed as white-collar workers; but 79.0% of those whose parents were both white-collar workers are so employed; and only 64.4% of those having fathers employed in white-collar jobs and mothers in manual work are so employed.

Other examples can be cited. Similarly, it becomes apparent that an equally strong influence on the individual's social status is exerted by the status of siblings. The probability of taking a job in a socioeconomic group other than that of one's parents increases considerably if an employed sibling has already done so, and it decreases substantially if the siblings remain in the parents' occupational group.

Summarizing the initial, most general conclusions: in spite of a natural tendency to "inherit" the social status defined by the position of all family members, there is a very large amount of social mobility from the individual-farm-owner group to both blue- and white-collar groups, and from the blue-collar to the white-collar group. The flow between the last two groups is not at all unilateral, however, and we must stress the fact, symptomatic of the blurring of intergroup boundaries, that one out of every four employed persons coming from white-collar families now does manual work.

The magnitude and general thrust of social mobility has changed in different periods depending on socioeconomic conditions. Thus, for example, the performance of white-collar work by persons of rural or blue-collar background occurred relatively more often in the years 1950-54 (being, of course, much rarer before the war) and shows a slight downward trend after 1955. The years 1950-54 were the period of constructing the centralized administration and of replacing the losses among the intelligentsia sustained during the war. At the same time, despite the building of a totally new socialist political and administrative structure, an exceptionally large number of persons having intelligentsia background also performed white-collar work during this period. The proportion performing such work was even larger than before the war. Among all people coming from the educated class who began their first job before the war, the percentage entering white-collar work was 58.0%. Whereas 62.9% of them do such work at present, the corresponding percentages for those starting their first job in the five-year period 1950-54 are 75.4% and 75.6% and show a definite downward trend in later years. This undoubtedly represents the effect of great demand for an educated work force in the beginning of the 1950s, one which resulted from entering a phase of accelerated economic growth accompanied by the construction of a new administrative system and by wartime losses in the educated population that were so difficult to replace during the first postwar years.

Although these figures represent all white-collar workers, we should note their agreement with education statistics concerning the creation of a qualified work force. The five years 1950-54 are marked by an unusually high number of college graduates (125,000 as compared to 36,000 in the years 1945-50, and 85,000 in the period 1956-60).

Changes in the mechanisms of recruitment to the working class were no less interesting. From the beginning of the second half of the fifties, we observe an increase in the percentage of workers of blue-collar origin who remain in the same socioeconomic group. At the same time, the percentage of blue-collar workers among individuals of white-collar origins shows a steady tendency to increase during this period. It rises from about 20% in the years 1950-54 to about 33% in the five-year period 1965-69 and in the last three survey years, 1970-72.

The incidence of manual workers among people of rural background rose systematically from the prewar period, when it was less than 15%, to the period 1960-64, when it exceeded 45%. During the next eight years it showed a slight tendency to decline in response to a trend toward remaining on self-owned farms. The trend to remain in individual farming emerged more clearly in the years 1970-72 and is doubtless associated with the new agricultural policy introduced in 1970.

Intergenerational Social Mobility

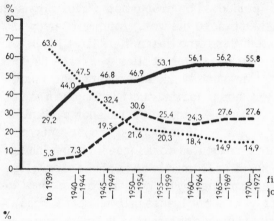

Figure 1.
All social origins
(total — 1972)

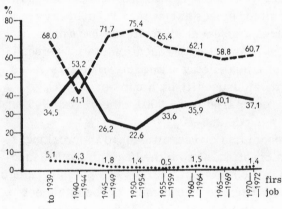

Figure 2.
Social origin:
intelligentsia
(fathers —
white-collar
workers)

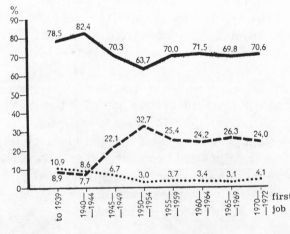

Figure 3.
Social origin:
worker
(fathers —
manual workers)

72

Changes in Social Structure and Mobility

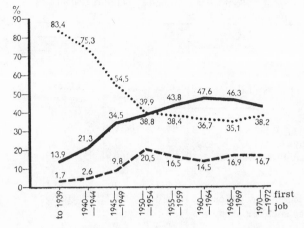

Figure 4.
Social origin:
peasant
(fathers —
individual
farmers)

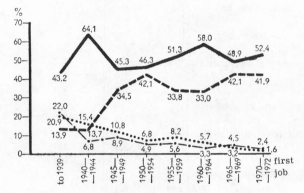

Figure 5.
Social origin:
petite bourgeoisie
(fathers —
self-employed
outside
agriculture)

Legend:
   Socioeconomic groups at the time of first employment:

   ———— manual workers
   - - - - nonmanual (white-collar) workers
   ·········· individual farmers
   ·—·—· self-employed outside agriculture

Note: In all figures those individuals whose first job was working
by contract or on commission were omitted because of their small
number. In Figures 1-4 those who first worked as self-employed
outside agriculture were omitted for the same reason.

Socio-occupational Groups in 1970-72 by

Socio-occupational groups of respondents	Total 1970[†]	Total 1972[‡]	Administrative and office workers
Total	100.0	100.0	100.0
Nonagricultural occupations	64.1	64.7	95.9
Workers and employees	61.6	62.7	94.1
Administrative and office workers	8.6	9.0	27.4*
Managers	0.9	0.9	2.4*
Others	7.7	8.1	25.0*
Specialists in technical occupations	4.0	4.8	16.6
Directors and technical or production managers	0.9	0.9	2.8
Other engineers, technicians and related staff	} 3.1	1.9	8.1
Master craftsmen and laboratory technicians		2.0	5.6
Specialists in nontechnical occupations	4.7	5.2	17.7
Higher level	—	3.4	12.7
Others	—	1.8	5.1
Workers in industrial and related occupations	} 25.3	23.3	16.7
Workers in construction and related occupations		2.9	1.1
Other manual workers	2.2	1.6	0.5
Workers in transport and communication	4.4	5.1	4.2
Employees in trade, storage, and nonindustrial services	5.9	6.6	6.8
Other service personnel‖	2.8	2.9	0.9
Self-employed#	1.3	1.2	0.8
In industrial, construction and related occupations	0.8	0.9	0.7
Working by contract and commission	1.2	0.8	0.9
Agricultural occupations, including forestry	35.8	35.3	4.1
Employees	2.8	2.8	1.5
Agricultural and forestry specialists	0.5	0.6	1.2
Agricultural and forestry workers, fishermen	2.3	2.2	0.3
Individual farmers#	32.8	32.5	2.6

*Refers to groups of persons who are in the same socio-occupational group as their fathers.

†Data of the National Census on working population (excluding the occupationally active having income other than earnings as main source of income).

Socio-occupational Groups of Fathers (in %)

Selected socio-occupational groups of fathers, 1972§						
Employees					Self-Employed	
Specialists in:		Blue-collar workers in:				
technical occupa-tions	nontech-nical oc-cupations	indus-try	construc-tion	agricul-ture and forestry	nonagri-cultural work	individual farmers
100.0	100.0	100.0	100.0	100.0	100.0	100.0
97.9	95.3	92.4	87.0	61.0	83.7	42.3
95.8	93.1	90.5	84.6	59.5	74.8	40.6
21.5	20.4	12.8	9.4	4.2	14.5	4.4
1.2	3.0	1.0	0.7	0.5	1.7	0.6
20.3	17.5	11.8	8.7	3.7	12.8	3.8
23.4*	17.2	7.3	3.9	2.1	6.8	2.0
3.4*	2.3	1.3	0.8	0.6	1.5	0.5
10.9*	9.2	2.7	1.4	0.7	2.7	0.6
9.0*	5.7	3.3	1.7	0.8	2.6	0.8
16.7	38.1*	5.9	3.3	2.0	7.9	2.7
12.5	32.0*	3.5	1.9	1.2	5.2	1.8
4.3	6.2*	2.4	1.4	0.9	2.7	0.9
17.7	8.7	40.2*	35.5	23.4	24.1	15.4
1.4	0.9	3.1	9.5*	4.1	2.9	2.4
0.5	0.4	1.5	2.1	2.4	1.1	1.5
4.1	2.5	5.8	6.8	6.4	4.9	4.1
6.7	3.2	9.2	8.6	8.0	8.2	4.8
1.0	0.4	3.2	4.2	5.1	2.8	2.4
1.3	1.5	0.9	1.1	0.9	7.7	0.9
0.7	0.7	0.6	0.9	0.7	6.4*	0.8
0.8	0.6	1.0	1.3	0.7	1.2	0.7
2.1	4.7	7.5	12.9	39.0	16.2	57.7
1.1	3.1	1.5	2.3	13.4	1.5	2.7
0.9	2.6	0.3	0.3	0.7	0.7	0.5
0.2	0.5	1.2	1.9	12.7*	0.8	2.2
1.0	1.6	6.0	10.7	25.5	14.7	55.0*

‡Survey data.
§At the time of respondent's first job.
‖Blue- and white-collar.
#Including supporting family members.

The intensity of flows between socioeconomic groups shows large variations over time. As we see, deviations do not occur in the same direction in all time periods. (The data are presented in Figures 1-5, pp. 72-73.)

Social Mobility between Socio-occupational Groups

Remaining within the same socioeconomic group by no means implies work in the same occupation or membership in the same socio-occupational milieu. For this reason, in studying social mobility it is not sufficient to use the basic classification of blue-collar and white-collar workers or other crude socioeconomic divisions.

Table 3 (pp. 74-75) contains information on the classification of the working population into socio-occupational groups and on socio-occupational origin as defined by father's position. In addition, the socio-occupational structures in 1970 (General Census) and in 1972 (present survey) are compared in the table. Considering the two-year gap between the two studies, as well as the incomplete overlap of the groupings, the data on the socio-occupational structure obtained in this survey should be considered reliable and wholly representative, since their direction agrees with general trends of change in the social structure and the differences are minimal.

We have already mentioned that one fourth of the persons from white-collar backgrounds are employed in manual work. The largest group of manual workers is laborers in industrial and related jobs. At the present time 16.7% of the sons and daughters of administrative-management and office workers are employed in industrial blue-collar work, as are 17.7% of the offspring of technical specialists; but only 8.7% of those coming from a background in nontechnical areas are so employed.

Thus those persons whose fathers were specialists in nontechnical fields work as industrial laborers half as frequently, and likewise work half as frequently at jobs that are borderline between blue- and white-collar categories (jobs in transport, communication, commerce, and nonindustrial services). More often, in almost 40% of the cases, they seek work in the same socio-occupational group as their fathers, and they also more frequently assume managerial positions.

The "exchange" between these three white-collar groups, that is, between specialists in technical areas, those in nontechnical fields, and administrative-office workers, is clearly apparent. Around 15-20% of the workers coming from each specific white-collar group work in each of the two remaining groups. Nonetheless, workers employed in their fathers' socio-occupational group are the single largest category in all three groups.

Much greater differences in the magnitude and direction of socio-occupational mobility occur among the three blue-collar groups discussed next.

Of the offspring of workers performing industrial and related jobs, 40.7% currently work in that same socio-occupational group, as do 9.5% of those from families of construction workers. Fourteen percent of those coming from families of agricultural and forestry workers are also self-recruited. We should note, however, that the three selected socio-occupational blue-collar groups differ greatly in size.

Workers in industrial and related jobs make up 23.3% of the labor force, while the number of construction workers and agricultural and forestry workers is one tenth as large (2.9% and 2.2%). To evaluate the magnitude of social mobility properly, the percentage of a given socio-occupational group from a specific social background should be compared with the percentage of this group in the total labor force.

From this point of view the percentages given above show that persons having fathers working as industrial and related laborers are almost twice as likely as the whole labor force to work in such jobs (40.2% and 23.3%). However, the percentage of workers in construction and related jobs whose fathers also performed this type of work is three times as high as in the total labor force (9.5% and 2.9%). The percentage of agricultural and forestry workers among respondents whose parents performed such work exceeds the corresponding percentage of the total labor force by a factor of six (14.0% and 2.2%).

Persons coming from families of industrial and related workers more often work in intelligentsia-type occupations than persons from construction-worker families, and the latter in turn more often than those from families of agricultural and forestry workers. A reverse trend occurs in the relationship between blue-collar origins and current affiliation with individual farming and the least-skilled labor groups, such as workers in various unskilled manual jobs and "residual service personnel" (e.g., porters, janitors, custodians, cleaning women, messengers, etc.).

Social Mobility between Occupational Groups

The data discussed above allow us to conclude that an appreciable increase in social mobility processes does not mean the total disappearance of the tendency to inherit status in the socio-occupational structure. This tendency is clearly apparent in an analysis of social mobility in terms of separation into both large socioeconomic groups and also into smaller, more precisely defined socio-occupational groups. The survey results also reveal a definite tendency to inherit specific occupations.

For example, we can state that whereas the percentage of doctors and dentists among the total population is 0.4%, their percentage among persons whose fathers were doctors and dentists amounts to 23.1%, i.e., more than fifty times as high. The corresponding figures for judges, prosecutors, attorneys, and representatives of related legal professions are 0.2% and 7.1%. This difference is much smaller, amounting only to a factor of thirty-five. For the academic group the percentages are 0.2% and 17.4% (differing by a factor of over eighty-five), and for the professional teachers group, 1.9% and 19.6% (differing by a factor of ten).

Similar trends, though of differing intensity, appear in most occupational groups, both white- and blue-collar. Thus maintaining the family's vocational tradition is a very common oc-

Changes in Social Structure and Mobility

currence in Poland. Undoubtedly it cannot be considered an
attribute only of traditional societies because it also appears
in modern societies, even those characterized by a relatively
high rate of social mobility.

General Tendencies and Directions of Change

For the last few years we have observed a leveling, and even
a slight downward trend, in mobility from working-class and
farming backgrounds to intelligentsia groups and a simultaneous
tendency toward the growth of coefficients of outflow from the
intelligentsia to the blue-collar groups. This signifies the end-
ing of the "extensive" growth in the availability of white-collar
jobs. Second, it signifies a change in the prestige ascribed to
the various groups and the attendant gradual decline of barriers
dividing the working class and the intelligentsia, especially
those between skilled workers and the middle and lower office
and technical work force.

The gradual shift from the extensive to the intensive mode
of economic development is also expressed in the emerging,
yet slight, downward trend in mobility from the individual
farmer group to the working-class groups. Of course other
factors also affect this phenomenon, for example, the unfavorable age structure in the individual farm work force and the increasing attractiveness of agriculture arising from new principles of farm policy introduced in the seventies. The limited
absorptive power of the cities and the rising cost of their development inhibit rural to urban migration and are also factors
in this emerging trend.

We must consider the fact that trends which are just beginning to emerge will intensify in the future, possibly with the
exception of decreasing mobility from blue-collar to white-
collar groups. An increasing demand for a specialized work
force will probably reverse this trend and produce an increase
in mobility from blue-collar to white-collar groups. This need
not imply, however, a simultaneous slowing down of the flow

79

from the intelligentsia to the blue-collar groups characteristic
of the majority of developed societies regardless of their political systems.

All these effects are closely related to the change in migration and to the general rise in education. Further analysis of
these preliminary results will concentrate on determining more
precisely the changes in social mobility between particular
socio-occupational groups, studying the relationships between
social mobility and migration or changes in the level of education, and determining the degree of differentiation in the socio-
occupational composition of families, which constitutes an important factor in social integration.

Krystyna Janicka

INTERGENERATIONAL MOBILITY IN CITIES*

Introduction

Intergenerational mobility is usually analyzed in terms of socio-occupational differentiation. Empirical studies consist mostly of determining the amount of movement and its patterns.[1] The basis for determining the magnitude and direction of intergenerational mobility is mobility tables, in which information on the occupations of fathers is contrasted with data on the current occupations of their sons.[2] On the basis of such tables each element of the structure, either socio-occupational groups or social classes, can be analyzed in two ways:

a) the outflow of individuals from a common background (defined by the father's position) into the socio-occupational categories occupied by these individuals at the time of the study;

b) the inflow of individuals from diverse social backgrounds to common socio-occupational categories in the present structure.

Thus, in accordance with these two possibilities, each socio-occupational group may be characterized either by means of its distributive potential or by its recruitment base. Moreover,

*From Krystyna Janicka, "Ruchliwosc międzypokoleniowa," in K. Słomczyński and W. Wesołowski, eds., Struktura i ruchliwość społeczna (Wrocław: Ossolineum, 1973), pp. 61-101. Abridgements and small editorial changes have been made by the editors with the author's consent.

intergenerational mobility of the form measured in the tables is in fact a synthesis of two types of flow: structural movement and exchange movement. Structural mobility defines changes in the positions of individuals which take place as a result of differences in the proportions of socio-occupational groups between two generations, whereas exchange mobility denotes changes in the positions of individuals consisting of substitution as a result of the vacating of positions in specific socio-occupational groups by those who do not "inherit" their fathers' positions.[3] A knowledge of the relative proportions of these two kinds of mobility seems necessary both for a more thorough description of the process itself and for a clearer understanding of the whole occupational structure.

In analyzing intergenerational mobility I shall concentrate on the outflow process, that is, the respondent leaving the father's position. Adopting this line of reasoning I intend to answer these questions.

1. What are the main patterns of mobility (a) taking into consideration narrow socio-occupational groups such as intelligentsia, technicians, or skilled workers; (b) taking into account social classes distinguished by the type of work performed (white-collar workers, intermediate categories, blue-collar workers)?

2. What is the amount of total mobility, and how do the relative proportions of structural and exchange mobility compare in the three cities studied, Łódź, Szczecin, and Koszalin?

3. How open is the social structure in each of the three towns in terms of the inheritance of fathers' positions?

4. How does the openness of the social structure compare for cohorts beginning work at various points in time, for instance, in the years 1945-46, 1947-50, 1951-54, and 1955-60?

The data for this study were collected in Łódź, Szczecin, and Koszalin as a result of a study on social stratification.[4] Their differing sizes and degrees of industrialization necessitated that each town be treated separately in the analysis. The historical similarity of the Western Territories may have had a unifying influence on the processes that interest the author.

Intergenerational Mobility in Cities

The question then arises whether intergenerational mobility
proceeded in the same way in Szczecin and Koszalin but differently in Łódź, a city in central Poland. I intend to deal with
this question as well in the present paper.

The Effect of Social Origin on Socio-occupational Status

Here we will be concerned with intergenerational changes in
both socio-occupational groups and social classes. In the first
case the discussion will be confined to "transitions" among
socio-occupational groups characteristic of the urban social
structure. Then social positions attained primarily by persons
originating in white-collar and blue-collar families will be described. A separate section will be devoted to respondents of
farmer origin. Tables 1 and 2 contain data pertaining to both
kinds of intergenerational change. The following conclusions
are drawn on the basis of data in Table 1:
1. Among all socio-occupational groups the highest degree
of intergenerational stability is shown by persons of intelligentsia background. In Łódź and Szczecin somewhat more than
half the respondents in this category maintain their father's
status (Łódź — 56.2%, Szczecin — 51.3%), but in Koszalin the
corresponding percentage is nearly 40%. In contrast to Łódź
and Szczecin, the sons of the intelligentsia in Koszalin are almost as likely to become office workers as to remain in the
intelligentsia.
2. In the case of the sons of office workers, intergenerational
stability is less common than among the sons of the intelligentsia, ranging from 17.8% to 27.5%. The difference between
sons of the intelligentsia and of office workers is particularly
pronounced in Łódź where it amounts to around 40%. At the
same time, the sons of office workers in Łódź become members
of the intelligentsia twice as frequently as they remain in their
category of origin. Furthermore, movement into the category
of service workers happens as frequently as inheritance of
father's position. In the towns of the Western Territories, both

Intergenerational Mobility among

Father's occupation	City	intelligentsia	office worker	techni-cian	service worker
Intelligentsia	Ł	56.2	12.5	12.5	—
	S	51.3	11.4	20.0	2.9
	K	38.6	30.8	11.5	3.8
Office worker	Ł	35.8	17.8	10.7	17.8
	S	23.5	23.5	19.7	3.9
	K	32.5	27.5	12.5	2.5
Technician	Ł	(3)	—	(3)	—
	S	13.6	13.6	18.2	9.1
	K	20.0	26.7	20.0	6.7
Service worker	Ł	13.1	9.9	16.4	8.2
	S	8.2	19.2	13.7	20.6
	K	2.9	34.2	8.6	2.9
Craftsman	Ł	11.2	8.7	3.1	11.8
	S	13.1	9.8	9.8	12.4
	K	12.2	25.6	10.8	6.8
Foreman	Ł	17.1	25.7	8.6	5.7
	S	(4)	(1)	(1)	—
	K	—	(1)	(2)	—
Skilled worker	Ł	7.6	11.7	7.0	10.5
	S	6.2	11.5	10.6	10.6
	K	13.8	9.2	13.8	6.2
Semiskilled worker	Ł	4.0	8.0	8.0	8.0
	S	8.2	14.8	6.6	16.4
	K	10.0	6.7	16.7	6.7
Unskilled worker	Ł	2.4	6.3	4.8	12.7
	S	5.9	9.2	6.7	15.1
	K	6.3	25.3	11.4	6.3
Farmer	Ł	6.7	5.8	2.9	16.3
	S	11.9	8.5	5.8	10.9
	K	12.6	19.8	8.2	15.8

*The category "other" and missing data were omitted from the calculations.

†Percentage not calculated due to small cell entries.

Intergenerational Mobility in Cities

1

Socio-occupational Groups (in %)

present occupation*					
crafts-man	fore-man	skilled worker	semi-skilled worker	unskilled worker	number in categories N = 100%
12.5	6.3	—	—	—	16
—	8.6	2.9	—	—	35
3.8	—	3.8	—	—	26
3.6	3.6	10.7	—	—	28
7.8	—	5.9	2.0	3.9	51
—	—	2.5	—	5.0	40
—	—	(2)	—	—	8[†]
—	—	9.1	4.5	—	22
13.3	—	—	—	—	15
1.6	3.3	41.0	1.6	3.3	61
4.1	5.5	21.9	4.1	—	73
2.9	5.7	14.2	5.7	2.9	35
14.3	7.5	24.8	7.4	5.0	161
14.4	2.6	19.0	5.2	5.2	153
8.1	1.4	14.8	5.4	8.1	74
11.4	2.9	14.3	—	5.7	35
—	—	(1)	—	—	7[†]
(1)	—	(3)	—	(1)	8[†]
4.7	11.1	36.9	4.7	2.9	171
6.2	2.7	27.5	11.5	3.5	113
4.6	7.7	21.6	3.1	6.2	65
—	8.0	36.0	8.0	16.0	25
—	4.9	29.4	6.6	3.3	61
3.3	3.3	10.0	13.3	16.7	30
4.8	10.3	36.5	6.3	12.7	126
5.9	4.2	26.1	9.2	7.6	119
5.1	—	17.7	7.6	10.1	79
10.1	8.7	24.0	7.2	14.4	208
5.8	4.1	23.8	11.2	9.2	294
2.7	1.1	12.0	6.6	8.7	184

movement into the intelligentsia and stability among the sons of office workers occur at approximately the same rate. The largest remaining component of change is movement in the category of technicians (Sczcecin — 19.7%, Koszalin — 12.5%).

3. The sons of technicians in Szczecin and Koszalin "inherit" their fathers' positions somewhat less often than do office workers. Among the former group only 20% maintain their positions of origin. In Łódź the tendency of the sons of technicians toward intergenerational stability is more pronounced; but due to the small size of this category, such a result may be the consequence of random deviations. In each of the three towns, among the sons of technicians one observes a definite gravitation to the intelligentsia and office workers.

4. Among the sons of service workers and craftsmen only a small percentage "inherit" their fathers' positions. The most "stabilized" group is found in Szczecin, where 20% of the sons of service workers have not changed social position. Almost all the variants of intergenerational mobility are represented in the case of these two background categories. However, the sons of service workers in Łódź decidedly gravitate to skilled work; in Koszalin, to office work; and similarly in Szczecin, to both of these socio-occupational groups. In Łódź and Szczecin the sons of craftsmen most often become skilled laborers, and in Koszalin they become office workers. Among foremen the "inheritance" of father's position is either a very rare phenomenon (Łódź — 2.9%), or it does not appear at all (as in Szczecin and Koszalin). Using the example of Łódź one can say that for sons of foremen the most frequent types of change in position are movement to the category of office workers; second, to the intelligentsia; and third, to the skilled worker category.

5. The sons of skilled workers in the towns of the Western Territories remain in their category of origin to approximately the same degree as sons of office workers. In Łódź, on the other hand, stability in this background category is more common and amounts to 36.9%. The remaining patterns of intergenerational mobility for skilled workers in the three towns include all the possible kinds of transitions. Since these do not

occur very frequently (not exceeding 13%), intergenerational stability for sons of skilled workers is prevalent.

6. Intergenerational stability occurs less frequently than certain types of position change in the case of sons of semiskilled workers and unskilled workers. Of the semiskilled workers, 8.0% to 13.3% remain in their category of origin, whereas 7.6% to 12.7% of unskilled workers do so. Respondents in these two occupational categories in Łódź and Szczecin most frequently become skilled laborers. The highest percentage of persons experiencing this mobility pattern is in Łódź, where 36.5% of sons of semiskilled and unskilled workers become skilled workers. It is difficult to determine a clearly predominant category of current occupation for sons of semiskilled workers in Koszalin. They undergo displacements in a variety of directions with similar probabilities. Sons of unskilled workers in Koszalin are most often represented among office workers (25.3%). This variety of change in socio-occupational position occurs three times more frequently than in Szczecin, and four times more often than in Łódź.

The analysis of intergenerational changes in socio-occupational affiliation for the three towns reveals the comparative mobility processes for residents of Koszalin, Łódź, and Szczecin. Two particular features of intergenerational mobility in the Koszalin population are: (a) a decidedly more frequent flow from almost all categories (with the exception of the sons of skilled and semiskilled workers) to office workers; and (b) a relatively smaller inflow to the skilled worker category of the sons of service workers, craftsmen, and semiskilled and unskilled workers. These two general trends, which characterize intergenerational mobility in Koszalin, reflect that city's socio-occupational structure and are directly related to the relative proportions of office workers and skilled workers present in the city.

A broader analysis of socio-occupational mobility patterns requires limiting oneself to observation of fewer, more basic job classifications. Table 2 presents the data that are a basis for an answer to the question: How are respondents who orig-

Krystyna Janicka

Table 2

Intergenerational Mobility among Social Classes (in %)

Class position of father	City	Class position of respondent			Number in categories N = 100%
		white-collar worker	intermediate category	blue-collar worker	
White-collar worker	Ł	71.2	19.2	9.6	52
	S	67.6	11.1	9.3	108
	K	74.1	7.4	4.9	81
Intermediate category	Ł	30.4	26.8	37.4	257
	S	36.9	28.7	28.0	233
	K	47.0	14.5	28.2	117
Blue-collar worker	Ł	21.2	26.4	49.4	322
	S	26.0	22.1	42.0	293
	K	39.0	14.4	34.5	174
Farmer	Ł	15.3	34.0	46.5	215
	S	26.2	20.7	44.3	294
	K	40.2	19.5	27.2	184

*The category "other" and missing data were omitted from the calculations.

inated in white-collar, blue-collar, and peasant families presently situated in the social structure? On the basis of the percentage distributions in Table 2, one observes that inheritance of father's socio-occupational position is the predominant mobility process for sons of white-collar workers. The trend toward intergenerational stability for sons of blue-collar workers in the heavily industrialized cities of Łódź and Szczecin does not hold for Koszalin. In Koszalin the main mobility path for blue-collar workers' sons is movement to white-collar jobs. Similarly, movement to the white-collar group is the most common pattern of change in social position for sons of farmers in this town. In Łódź and Szczecin, on the other hand, the sons of farmers exhibit a propensity to become blue-collar workers.

Differences in the degree to which sons of farmers flow into white-collar jobs (15.3% in Łódź; 40.2% in Koszalin) are in large part caused by the existing job structure in each of the three towns. In Koszalin and Szczecin there are proportion-

ately more white-collar positions than in Łódź, and consequently movement into this social class is made easier in these
two towns of the Western Territories. Appreciable differences
among the cities also exist in terms of the outflow of sons of
blue-collar workers to white-collar occupations and to intermediate levels of the socio-occupational structure. The data
show that from 21% to 39% of the sons of blue-collar workers
move to white-collar jobs, and from 14% to 26% move to the
intermediate category.

Structural mobility is the consequence of changes in proportions of the various socio-occupational groups between the two
generations. In the literature it is stressed that the qualitative
and quantitative modifications of the socio-occupational structure are a consequence of the changing demand for various
types of jobs and various kinds of qualifications.[5] Independently
of these structural transitions, however, the interchange of individuals among socioeconomic groups characterizing comparable structures also takes place across generations. This substitution process occurs because some individuals do not maintain or do not achieve the qualifications necessary to remain
in the socio-occupational position occupied by their fathers,
and so they are "replaced" by persons from other origins who
are able to attain the necessary qualifications. Exchange mobility is defined as that portion of total change in socio-occupational positions between two generations that is independent of
structural change.

Although it is not possible to determine the type of mobility
experienced by a single individual, for the whole population we
are not only able to differentiate between the structural and exchange processes, but also to determine the magnitude of each.
The magnitude of structural and exchange mobility may be determined both absolutely and relative to total mobility.

The amount of total mobility is measured by summing the
values of all off-diagonal elements in a mobility table and then
expressing that sum as a percentage of total cases. In the first
row of Table 3 we can see that the amount of mobility is very
similar in the three towns; it varies from 71.2% to 78.7%. A

Table 3

Total Mobility and Its Components Classified by
Socio-occupational Groups (in %)

Type of mobility	Łódź	Szczecin	Koszalin
Total	71.2	76.3	78.4
Structural	33.0	41.2	40.7
Exchange	38.2	35.1	38.0
$\dfrac{\text{Structural}}{\text{Total}} \times 100$	46.4	54.0	51.7
$\dfrac{\text{Exchange}}{\text{Total}} \times 100$	53.6	46.0	48.3
Expected total mobility predicted by the equal opportunity model	74.8	82.0	82.4
$\dfrac{\text{Total mobility}}{\text{Expected total mobility in the equal opportunity model}} \times 100$	95.0	93.0	98.0

marked similarity among towns is also observed when the
amount of total mobility is compared with that predicted by the
equal opportunity model. The relationship of total observed
mobility to the expected values of the equal opportunity model
is expressed in the last row of Table 3. It appears from these
values that the amount of total intergenerational mobility is
quite similar in Łódź and both towns of the Western Territories
and, furthermore, departs only slightly from the expected values of the equal opportunity model.

As mentioned above, the amount of structural mobility is determined by changes in the sizes of the socio-occupational
groups between the generations of fathers and sons. The technological development of societies and accompanying modifications of the social structure are the primary sources of this
kind of change. However, it is obvious that demographic factors such as migration and socio-occupational differences in
net fertility rates also contribute to this change.

The amount of structural mobility tells us what percentage
of sons cannot inherit their fathers' positions for the sole reason that there are fewer jobs in certain occupational groups in

the sons' generation than in the fathers' generation. For example, if in Łódź in the fathers' generation the category of unskilled workers numbered 126 persons, and in the sons' generation, 90 people, then 36 people are "forced" to move into other categories. The craftsmen category in our study exhibits this feature. The sons of farmers are in a unique situation: because they live in the city, they have been "forced" to change their original socio-occupational affiliation. This contingency arises because the group of farmers does not have an equivalent in the population of sons, since we are considering the socio-occupational structure of large cities.

In the preceding example three of the socio-occupational categories specified, unskilled workers, craftsmen, and farmers, determine the magnitude of structural mobility. In the Łódź population the remaining occupational categories increase over the time separating the two generations. As we see in the second row of Table 3, structural mobility affects 33.0% of the Łódź population, 41.2% of the Szczecin population, and 40.7% of the Koszalin population. This mobility, as noted above, results from changes in such socio-occupational categories as intelligentsia, office workers, technicians, and skilled workers, and from the absence of farming occupations in the population studied.

It is easy to see that the magnitude of total mobility considerably exceeds structural mobility. The difference between total mobility and structural mobility is referred to as exhange mobility. From the third line of Table 3 we note that in Łódź and Koszalin the levels of exchange mobility are identical (38.0%), whereas in Szczecin the level is slightly lower (35.1%). Thus, as in the case of structural mobility, we do not observe substantial differences among the towns.

However, considering structural and exchange mobility as proportions of total mobility, their relative importance is different in Łódź than in both cities of the Western Territories. As seen in lines 4 and 5 of Table 3, in Szczecin and Koszalin structural mobility exceeds exchange mobility, whereas in Łódź the reverse is true. The differences noted between the

towns are not large enough, however, for us to justifiably conclude that there exists some specific, local composition of the
two components of mobility. Since reliance on a detailed breakdown on the socio-occupational structure reveals no pronounced
differences between the towns, this question will be reconsidered
in the context of more broadly defined social classes.

The data given in Table 4 represent the level of total mobility
as well as its structural and exchange components, which result from the flow of individuals among social classes: white-
collar workers, intermediate categories, blue-collar workers,
and farmers. A comparison of the corresponding values in lines
1 through 3 in Tables 3 and 4 shows how two interpretations of
the social structure (according to socio-occupational groups or
according to social classes) modify the quantitative picture of
social mobility. With a more general treatment, that is, in
terms of social classes, the level of total mobility and its structural component become considerably lower, but the level of
exchange mobility does not exhibit appreciable change. If in
total mobility among social classes we examine the proportions
of the structural and exchange components, the differences be-

Table 4

Total Mobility and Its Components
Classified by Social Classes (in %)

Type of Mobility	Łódź	Szczecin	Koszalin
Total	57.2	63.0	66.2
Structural	20.8	28.0	33.2
Exchange	36.4	35.0	33.0
$\dfrac{\text{Structural}}{\text{Total}} \times 100$	36.4	44.4	50.1
$\dfrac{\text{Exchange}}{\text{Total}} \times 100$	63.6	55.6	49.9
Expected total mobility predicted by the equal opportunity model	61.4	70.0	72.2
$\dfrac{\text{Total mobility}}{\text{Expected total mobility in the equal opportunity model}} \times 100$	93.0	90.0	92.0

tween Łódź and the two cities of the Western Territories turn out to be higher than in the case of mobility among socio-occupational groups.

In the more general treatment of the urban social structure in Łódź, exchange mobility constitutes two thirds of total mobility, but in the towns of the Western Territories the proportions of both types of flow are nearly equal. On this basis one can say that whereas in Łódź, Szczecin, and Koszalin total mobility is about the same, the proportion of exchange mobility to that of structural mobility is clearly higher in Łódź than in the population of the Western cities. Thus if one were to take as the index of openness of social structure the magnitude of mobility independent of structural changes, Łódź would appear to be more open than the towns of the Western Territories studied.

Openness of Socio-occupational Groups and Social Classes

In the literature on mobility one finds the suggestion that the level of exchange mobility be treated as an index of the openness of society.[6] Furthermore it is emphasized that from a sociological point of view the phenomenon that goes beyond structural requirements is more interesting than the one that inevitably results from the objective character of the structure. Focusing on the movement of individuals that is independent of structural changes allows us to draw conclusions about the character and scope of interaction of various psychological and social mechanisms that regulate the allocation of persons into socio-occupational groups and social classes. Also important is the fact that the definition of the degree of openness of the social structure makes possible a comparison of a variety of structures with differing rates of technological and demographic change.

In the preceding section data were cited indicating a certain differentiation among cities in the contribution of exchange mobility to total mobility. Therefore we can say that the cities differ with respect to the openness of their structures. In order to evaluate the significance of these differences, it is essential to apply an appropriate measure of the relative intensity of exchange mobility. The proposed measure is the openness coefficient Y.

This index has the following form:[7]

$$Y_{ii} = (\bar{n}_{ii} - f_{ii})/(\bar{n}_{ii} - \frac{n_{i.} \cdot n_{.i}}{N}),$$

where:

$n_{i.}$ — the number of fathers in a given category;

$n_{.i}$ — the number of sons in a given category;

$\bar{n}_{ii}$ — the smaller of the values $n_{i.}$ and $n_{.i}$;

f_{ii} — the number of sons in the same category as their fathers;

N — total sample size.

The formula as presented allows one to calculate the magnitude of exchange mobility not only for specific categories of social origin, but also for the whole social structure. In the latter case the coefficient has the following form:

$$Y = \left(\sum \bar{n}_{ii} - \sum f_{ii}\right) / \left(\sum \bar{n}_{i.} - \sum \frac{n_{i.} \cdot n_{.i}}{N}\right).$$

Calculated for all the categories taken together, the Y coefficient is a synthetic measure making it possible to characterize the openness of the structure. In calculating the Y coefficient the position each of the categories considered might have in a hierarchy does not matter. Therefore this coefficient is not an index of advancement or demotion.[8]

Table 5

Openness of Social Classes

Social class	Łódź	Szczecin	Koszalin
	Y coefficient		
White-collar workers	0.38	0.48	0.47
Intermediate categories	1.01	0.92	0.99
Blue-collar workers	0.90	0.90	0.90
Urban social structure	0.90	0.84	0.85

94

Intergenerational Mobility in Cities

Table 5 shows the Y coefficients for Łódź, Szczecin, and Koszalin. These coefficients express the openness of specific social classes and of the entire urban social structure.

From these data it appears that the degree of openness of the entire structure of the towns is very high and markedly close to the equal opportunity model ($Y_L = 0.90$, $Y_S = 0.84$, $Y_K = 0.85$). Slight differences, however, show that in the social structures of Szczecin and Koszalin the barriers separating social classes are not more elastic than in Łódź. The almost-identical degree of openness of the social structures of Łódź, Szczecin, and Koszalin is thought-provoking. It suggests the existence of universal factors, or superlocal selection systems, which regulate and standardize the exchange mobility process between generations in the large cities of Poland.

In all three cities white-collar workers are characterized by relatively little exchange of individuals. Differences between cities indicate that in Szczecin ($Y_S = 0.48$) and in Koszalin ($Y_K = 0.47$) the fact of having come from the white-collar class is less connected with structural stability than in Łódź ($Y_L = 0.38$). However, in each of the towns the degree of openness of the blue-collar class is identical and shows that the exchange of individuals between this class and the remaining classes takes place at a level approaching the equal opportunity model.

The fact that white-collar jobs are characterized by less openness than blue-collar jobs requires interpretation. In explaining the considerable weakening of exchange in the case of white-collar workers, we should take into account two kinds of factors: (1) motivation and aspiration, and (2) life chances. It is to be expected that among sons of white-collar workers, the motivations and aspirations to maintain oneself in that work group would be quite strong. Moreover, persons in this category usually have more favorable conditions for obtaining those attributes essential to maintain the positions held by their fathers.

Openness of the Urban Social Structure
in Dynamic Perspective

In the analysis so far the basis for describing intergenerational mobility was a comparison of the present position of the respondents with the position of their fathers. When the objective is to describe the dynamics of the social structure, one must perform an analysis of age cohorts, because respondent's age and duration of occupational career affect his present social position. Older groups, having objectively greater possibilities of changing position in the course of a professional career, could exhibit a higher level of intergenerational mobility than younger groups. In order to eliminate the effect of intragenerational mobility, I will compare the respondent's first job with his father's occupation.

Drawing conclusions about the openness of the urban social structure over a longer period of time requires that we limit ourselves to that part of the population which resided in the given city during the whole period of interest. Since the possibilities of controlling the place of respondent's initial employment are better in Łódź, I will confine analysis of the openness of urban social structure to that city. In Table 6 we have values of the openness coefficient for the period of initial employment for those people whose first job was in Łódź. These data provide information on the level of relative exchange mobility in

Table 6

Openness of Social Classes in Łódź
Classified by Period of Initial Employment

Period of initial employment	Social class			Urban social structure
	white-collar workers	intermediate categories	blue-collar workers	
	Y coefficient			
Before the war	0.68	0.85	0.61	0.72
1945-46	0.40	0.95	0.69	0.72
1947-50	0.58	1.01	0.98	0.91
1951-54	0.62	1.02	0.82	0.88
1955-60	0.55	0.69	0.60	0.61
1961 and later	~0	1.34	0.81	0.81

six time periods: before the war, 1945-46, 1947-50, 1951-55, 1956-60, as well as 1961 and after.

Openness indices for the whole social structure of Łódź, calculated for different time periods, do not fall into an ordered sequence of increasing values. The tendency to inherit social position in successive generations is subject to fluctuation. The highest level of relative exchange mobility characterized the social structure of Łódź in the years 1947-50. The degree of mobility for the generation entering the labor market in the period immediately after the war (1945-46) was identical to the level of mobility of the older generation.[9] The least openness occurs in the years 1955-60, in which a rather considerable stiffening of the social structure took place. Most strongly affected were individuals of working-class background and the intermediate category.

What can explain the increased importance of social background in determining initial employment in the years 1955-60? It is sometimes said that in the second half of the 1950s the role of nonmerit criteria in the process of employment recruitment was reduced. In view of the stronger emphasis on occupational training, the likelihood of social advancement, which was rather strong in the period of the reconstruction of the country and extensive industrialization, became weakened. It may be that changes in aspirations were also important.

The data in Table 6, apart from information on the general level of exchange mobility, indicate the openness of each of three social classes: white-collar workers, blue-collar workers, and the intermediate categories. In the case of white-collar workers the sequence of values of the openness coefficient for successive periods shows considerable fluctuation. If we compare this with the level of openness that characterized the oldest group of Łódź residents, we see that the openness of white-collar jobs after the war departs from the equal opportunity model to a greater degree than before the war. A particular stiffening of barriers "shielding" this social class occurs in the period immediately after the war and at the beginning of the 1960s. This indicates that sons of white-collar workers who began employment in Łódź in those two periods started in non-white-collar occupations much less frequently than the older generations. Increased self-recruitment of these categories, particularly characteristic in the years 1961-65, seems to indicate a serious limitation of psychological mechanisms that stimulated the inflow of young people from blue-collar families or from intermediate categories to the white-collar class. It is debatable whether this stabilization of the social structure is desirable.

The blue-collar class shows a greater increase in openness than the white-collar class, although, as for the latter, the values of the openness coefficient do not increase monotonically over time. The change in social position of persons of blue-collar origin most closely approaches the model of equal opportunity for the years 1947-50. However, for the ten-year period 1950-60 there is a decrease in openness. In this period the sons of blue-collar workers, while taking their first job more frequently in response to objective opportunities, remained in their class of origin. After 1961 one can speak again of a rise in openness. However, it does not exceed its maximum, which occurred in the years 1947-50.

An analysis of the extent of exchange mobility, defined by class positions, leads to several summary observations:

1. Openness of the urban social structure does not increase monotonically over time. Therefore the influence of social origin on class position, independent of structural factors, does not decrease with time.

2. The most appreciable rise in openness of the social structure of Łódź occurred in the years 1947-50. In this period the influence of social origin on the class position attained at the initial job was weakest and came closest to the equal opportunity model.

3. After 1950 there emerged a tendency to stiffen the barriers separating social classes, with the strongest relationship between social origin and first job occurring in the years 1955-60.

4. The relative magnitude of exchange mobility for those who began employment after 1960 shows a tendency toward

more openness for the social structure as a whole. This trend
does not encompass the white-collar class, which in this period
was characterized by almost complete self-recruitment.

Conclusion

The object of the present study was not only a conventional
description but also an analytic treatment of social mobility in
terms of its components: structural and exchange mobility.
The need for such a distinction seems obvious, since each of
the components of mobility is concerned with a different type
of change in the social structure and is an expression of different aspects of the structure. Structural mobility is an adaptation to technological and demographic changes, whereas exchange mobility demonstrates the degree of egalitarianism reg-
ulating the exchange of individuals among socioeconomic groups
and social classes.

A specific analytical model was used in the analysis, one that
stresses the process of individual exchange. The essence of
the model is a comparison of the actual exchange of individuals
with the magnitude that should occur in an equal opportunity
situation. The openness coefficient allows one to measure the
intensity of relative exchange mobility.

Let us recall that mobility affects a sizeable percentage of
the population in the three towns. Taking the three towns together, it affects from 57.2% to 66.2% of the samples. In Łódź
structural mobility accounts for twice as much total mobility
as does exchange mobility, whereas for Szczecin and Koszalin
the proportions are about equal. The intensity of relative exchange mobility reveals the similarity of the three cities with
respect to the degree of openness of the social structure as a
whole. Furthermore, this degree of openness is quite close to
the level predicted by the equal opportunity model ($Y_L = 0.90$,
$Y_S = 0.84$, $Y_K = 0.85$).

The openness coefficient has been used in the study of mobility in other countries. Since these studies were based on

nationwide samples, they are not completely comparable with the results presented here. Nonetheless, for the purposes of orientation it seems interesting to compare our results with them. From Yasuda's data it appears that among the countries considered, Great Britain has the most open social structure, whereas France has the lowest level of intergenerational exchange mobility.[10] The values of the openness coefficient calculated for Szczecin and Koszalin are equal to the highest values given by Yasuda, and in Łódź they exceed it. We must keep in mind, however, that the indices obtained from our data pertain only to the populations of selected cities where, it can be supposed, mobility is higher than the national average. How well values for these cities represent national trends in Poland remains an open question.

In the present article I was also concerned with a dynamic interpretation of the openness of the social structure. This approach required elimination of the possible influence of intragenerational mobility on present class position. To do this an analysis of the relation between class position during initial employment and class position of father was undertaken. On the basis of the Łódź example, it was found that the openness of the urban social structure has not increased uniformly over time.

Notes

1. O. D. Duncan briefly discussed various measures of mobility in his article "Methodological Issues in the Analysis of Social Mobility," in N. J. Smelser and S. M. Lipset, eds., Social Structure and Mobility in Economic Development (Chicago: Aldine, 1966).

2. Despite methodological drawbacks of this treatment, the comparison of the principal occupation of the father with the occupation of the respondent at the time of the study is universally used in studies of intergenerational mobility.

3. The term "inheriting" is applied in the present text interchangeably with the concept of "stability."

4. Editors' note: The study covered working men 21-65 years of age who were family heads. Interviews were conducted among 630 residents

Intergenerational Mobility in Cities

of Koszalin and 1,051 residents of Szczecin in 1964, and with 1,000 residents of Łódź in 1965. Representative samples were picked by systematic sampling from the files of city residents in Koszalin and Szczecin and from the voting registers in Łódź. See K. M. Słomczyński and W. Wesołowski, "Próby reprezentacyjne i kategorie społeczno-zawodowe," in W. Wesołowski, ed., Zróżnicowanie społeczne (Wrocław: Ossolineum, 1970).

5. Compare, e.g., J. A. Kahl, The American Class Structure (New York: Holt, Rinehart, and Winston, 1957).

6. N. Rogoff Ramsey, "Changes in Rates and Forms of Mobility," in N. J. Smelser and S. M. Lipset, eds., op. cit.

7. S. Yasuda, "A Methodological Inquiry into Social Mobility," American Sociological Review 29(1964), 16-23.

8. Only in the case of extreme categories of this stratification scheme does the general outflow of sons have the unambiguous character of advancement or demotion.

9. The similarity of these two periods in terms of openness of the social structure may be caused to a certain extent by the lack of precise information on the first occupation of persons who began to work before the war.

10. S. Yasuda, "A Methodological Inquiry into Social Mobility."

Kazimierz Słomczyński

THE ROLE OF EDUCATION IN THE PROCESS OF INTRAGENERATIONAL MOBILITY*

Introductory Remarks

In recent years an increasing number of papers have analyzed various factors that affect the socio-occupational status of individuals at particular points in their careers.[1] Among papers of this genre studies of the role of education have a distinct place.[2] In this paper I will examine to what degree the education of individuals produces changes in their occupational status. In particular I will concern myself with the effect which increasing the level of education during the course of one's occupational career has on possible social advancement. This question seems equally important from the theoretical and practical points of view.

Data contained in this article are taken from a survey conducted in Łódź in 1965.[3] In principle we will utilize information on four variables characterizing respondents. They are:

1. socioeconomic status at the time of first employment;
2. socioeconomic status at the time of most recent employment;
3. education before beginning first employment;

---

*From Kazimierz Słomczyński, "Rola wykształcenia w procesie ruchliwości wewnątrzpokoleniowej," in K. Słomczyński and W. Wesołowski, eds., Struktura i ruchliwość społeczna (Wrocław, Ossolineum, 1973), pp. 103-23.

4. change in education between first and most recent employment.

Comparison of first and most recent employment is a measure of the intragenerational occupational mobility of individuals. In turn, comparing the difference in educational level before first employment and at most recent employment provides information on "educational mobility." Thus the chosen set of variables allows us to answer various questions concerning the interrelations between both of these types of social mobility.

The treatment of the variable "socio-occupational status" requires some comment. Ordinarily the division of people into socio-occupational groups is differentiated horizontally. Applying this conceptual framework, one cannot say whether a given individual is situated at a higher, identical, or lower level relative to other individuals. In connection with this it is stressed that socio-occupational groups can only be treated as a nominal variable.[4]

It is worth noting that socio-occupational groups can be characterized by means of a series of variables closely correlated with the nature of work involved. Wage income or occupational prestige are good examples of this. Precisely on the basis of such vertical correlates, we are able to determine general hierarchies of socio-occupational groups. In this study we have used one such scale constructed from an index of education, work responsibility, income, and prestige.[5]

The hierarchy appears as follows:

intelligentsia — 95
technicians — 86
office workers — 74
masters and foremen — 63
artisans — 57
skilled workers — 43
service workers — 30
semiskilled workers — 21
unskilled laborers — 11.

The scores next to each socio-occupational group are treated here as measures of the socio-occupational positions of respondents.[6] Although the whole hierarchy contains certain elements of subjectivity, thorough examination of previous work in the area of scaling indicates that this index seems to be an appropriate measure.

Using this specific point system for socio-occupational positions and taking the number of grades finished in school as an indicator of educational level permits the use of statistical techniques appropriate for interval variables. In this treatment we will use correlation and regression analysis in order to describe various kinds of social mobility processes.[7]

The Effect of First Employment on
Present Socio-occupational Status

This part of the paper is devoted to the possibility of predicting the present socio-occupational positions of the respondents on the basis of the positions they held when first employed. The analysis will be conducted using cohorts that will denote different historical time periods during which the individuals' occupational careers began. The time intervals and sizes of the cohorts considered were:

cohort I: before 1946 — 626
cohort II: 1946-50   — 182
cohort III: 1951-55   — 122
cohort IV: 1956-60   — 70

The first cohort includes a large proportion of people (64.0%) who began work before 1939. That is, some individuals in our sample began their occupational careers even before the war. It is obvious that at that time the general socio-occupational hierarchy was different than after the war. Unfortunately we do not have at hand any data on the status distances between occupations in this period, and only such data would be applicable in this analysis. For the purposes of this study, therefore, we have decided to use the occupation in which the respondents worked in 1945 as the measure of the first job. This tactic

Education and Intragenerational Mobility

seems justified in view of the political and economic transformations that occurred in Polish society during the period just
after the war. One can say that in a sense even those who had
already been working before the war began their occupational
careers again after the war.

On the basis of data in Table 1, we can conclude that across
cohorts the average socio-occupational starting positions were
rather similar. The average scores of individual cohorts indicate this: 44.2; 44.6; 45.8; 46.7. Although the differences between cohorts are not large, it is still worthwhile to emphasize
a certain trend: those who began their work later started in
somewhat higher positions. Presumably this was caused by
changes in the occupational structure and the creation of an
ever increasing number of new positions requiring higher qualifications.

Table 1

Mean Value of Socio-occupational Status
during Initial and Present Employment

Items measured	Time of beginning first employment			
	before 1946	1946-50	1951-55	1956-60
Arithmetic mean of socio-occupational status at time of first employment (P)	44.2	44.6	45.8	46.7
Arithmetic mean of socio-occupational status during present employment (O)	48.3	49.8	51.6	49.6
Difference (O – P)	4.1	5.2	5.8	2.9
Percentage of respondents experiencing upward mobility	31.1	35.6	34.9	24.4
Percentage of stable respondents	53.3	51.1	55.0	59.0
Percentage of respondents experiencing downward mobility	15.6	13.3	11.1	15.6

In each cohort the arithmetic mean score for present position is higher than the analogous measure referring to the position held during the period of first employment. These differences range from 2.5 to 5.8 points and are rather moderate. They signify, however, that in all cohorts the sum of displacements to higher positions is greater than the sum of displacements to lower positions, which can be interpreted as a predominance of upward mobility. On the average the persons who began employment in the postwar period, 1946-55, advanced the most. These respondents had 10-20 years of work experience and were generally 30-40 years old. As to be expected, these persons were at the peak of their occupational careers.

The smallest average advancement is to be found in the case of respondents who began work either before 1946 or in the years 1956-60. It is probable that the former reached the ceiling of their occupational possibilities even earlier and at present show some tendency to downward mobility; however, the others still have this ceiling before them. In any case, a more penetrating analysis of the results should also take into account the variables of age and duration of employment.[8]

There is more difference between cohorts in average present positions than in their average starting positions. This greater intercohort differentiation of present position shows not only the effect of age and work qualification but also of historical conditions surrounding the start and development of careers. On the average the highest positions were achieved by those who began their first job between 1951 and 1955. Thus at a time of considerable social mobility, the advancement of this whole group was relatively rapid, for by 1960 their average score was already 49.9, only 0.2 less than it was in 1955.

Using this hierarchy of socio-occupational groups, upward mobility processes affected from 24.4% to 35.6% of the respondents depending on the period of initial employment. Of this sample, 51.1-59.0% are stable individuals, i.e., those who remained in their original socio-occupational group. Thus downward processes of mobility are small.

Let us now proceed to the regression analysis. The data

Table 2

Present Socio-occupational Position (O) Regressed on
Socio-occupational Status during First Employment (P)

Items	Period of beginning initial employment			
measured	before 1946	1946-50	1951-55	1956-60
Arithmetic mean, $\overline{O}$	48.3	49.8	51.6	49.6
Arithmetic mean, $\overline{P}$	44.2	44.6	45.8	46.7
Standard deviation, S_O	23.1	24.4	26.1	27.0
Standard deviation, S_p	22.8	25.1	26.8	26.9
Constant, a	18.7	18.0	16.0	11.3
Slope of the regression line, b_{op}	0.603	0.700	0.778	0.851
Correlation coefficient, r_{op}	0.597	0.719	0.798	0.847
Explained variance O, in %	35.6	51.7	63.7	71.7
a $(1-b_{op})$	46.4	64.0	79.1	75.3

needed for this are contained in Table 2. Before we discuss
the results, it is worthwhile to recall some assumptions underlying the application of regression analysis to our data.[9] If in
each cohort the position at the time of first employment (denoted by P) was the same as the position held at the time of the
study (denoted by O), then the arithmetic mean of O would be
equal to the mean of P, the standard deviations of both variables
would be equal, and the slope of the regression line as well as
the correlation coefficient would be unity.

We have already recalled the differences in the arithmetic
means of both variables. In Table 2 we see that for all cohorts
only the standard deviations of both variables are similar. The
correlation coefficients do not equal unity, which means that
the slopes of the regression lines are less than 1. This "regression to the mean" expresses a tendency toward socio-
occupational stability. The slope of the regression line, expressed as the coefficient b_{op}, indicates that the closer the period of first employment to the time of the survey, the stronger
the tendency toward stability.

The magnitudes of the correlation coefficients show that explained variance in the dependent variable ranges from 35.6% in cohort I to 71.7% in cohort IV. Generally we can better predict the present position of individuals if their occupational careers have begun recently. Among other reasons this is due to the tendency toward socio-occupational stability, which is in turn related to the smaller possibilities younger persons, employed for a shorter time, have for changing their positions.

Regression analysis also allows an interpretation of data in the categories of upward and downward mobility. It follows from the principle of regression toward the mean that upward mobility is a common pattern for persons with a relatively low starting position, while downward mobility is likely for persons with a relatively high starting position. A graphic illustration of this effect will facilitate further analysis (see Figure 1).

The OP plane may be represented in such a way that present occupation is plotted along the vertical axis, and initial occupation lies on the horizontal. If we draw line $O = P$ on the plane, all points situated to the right of the line will represent people who were downwardly mobile. If the observed regression line is given by the equation $O = a + bP$, we might find its point of intersection with the line $O = P$. This point where the abscissa and the ordinate are equal to $a(1-b)$ indicates the value of P below which downward mobility is the average occurrence. In Figure 1 these two magnitudes are given by the segments k and l.

Let us review the results presented in the last row of Table 2. We see, for example, that in cohort I the expression $a(1-b)$ has a value of 46.4, which means that for persons who obtained a lower initial score, the average mobility pattern is upward. Since the score of each individual corresponds to a specific socio-occupational group, we now move on to an analysis of these groups.

It is easy to discern that in cohort I the score indicating upward mobility (that is, lower than 46.4) belonged to skilled workers, service workers, semiskilled laborers, and unskilled laborers. In cohort II we add to these four groups artisans and masters and foremen; in cohort III, office workers; and in

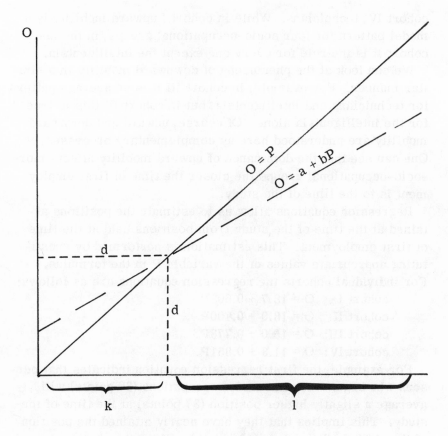

Figure 1. Geometrical interpretation of the occupational mobility process.

P — initial socio-occupational position;

O — present socio-occupational position;

d $= \dfrac{a}{1-b}$, where a and b are the appropriate expressions for the regression equation;

k — values of variable P for which the average values of variable O indicate an "upward" mobility;

l — values of the P variable for which the average values of the variable O indicate "downward" mobility.

cohort IV, technicians. While in cohort I upward mobility is a
model pattern for four socio-occupational groups, in the last
cohort it is the rule for every one except the intelligentsia.

We can look at the phenomena of downward mobility in a similar manner. For example, in cohort III it is an average pattern
for technicians and intelligentsia, but in cohort IV this is true
for the intelligentsia alone. Of course, upward and downward
mobility are understood here as complementary processes.
One can see that the dominance of upward mobility affects more
socio-occupational groups the closer the time of first employment is to the time of the study.

Regression equations allow us to estimate the positions attained at the time of the study from positions held at the time
of first employment. This estimation is performed by substi-
tuting appropriate values of the variable P in the formulas.
For individual cohorts the regression equations are as follows:

cohort I: $O = 18.7 + 0.603P$
cohort II: $O = 18.0 + 0.700P$
cohort III: $O = 16.0 + 0.778P$
cohort IV: $O = 11.3 + 0.851P$.

For example, the first regression equation indicates that persons who began work in service occupations (30 points) will
average a slightly higher position (37 points) at the time of the
study. This implies that they have nearly attained the position
of the skilled labor group (43 points). Of course, in the case of
each socio-occupational group these estimated values can be
compared with the actual values, and we can check how possible
deviations are distributed. This operation has been carried
out for the largest cohort in Table 3.

Overall the estimated values are in agreement with the actual
values, since for six groups the error does not exceed 10%.
Substantially larger deviations appear only in extreme groups,
the intelligentsia and the unskilled laborers. In both these
cases the estimated values are lower than the actual values,
which means that the actual mobility process is favorable for
these groups. Technicians, semiskilled workers, and skilled
workers are in a similar position, although the level of devia-

110

Education and Intragenerational Mobility

Table 3

Comparison of Average Observed and Expected Values
of Current Socio-occupational Status (O) in the Cohort
That Began Work before 1946

Socio-occupational status during first employment	Observed value O_o	Expected value O_e	Difference $(\overline{O}_o - \overline{O}_e)$	Ratio $\dfrac{\overline{O}_o}{\overline{O}_e} \times 100$
Intelligentsia	89.9	75.7	+ 14.1	84.3
Technicians	74.8	70.3	+ 4.5	94.0
Office workers	59.2	63.1	− 3.9	106.6
Masters and foremen	58.2	56.5	+ 1.7	97.1
Artisans	48.3	52.8	− 4.5	109.3
Skilled workers	46.5	44.5	+ 2.0	95.7
Service workers	38.4	36.7	+ 1.7	95.6
Semiskilled workers	35.4	31.3	+ 4.1	88.4
Unskilled workers	32.8	25.3	+ 7.5	77.1

tion from predicted values is much smaller. The estimated
values are somewhat higher than the actual values for the office
worker and artisan groups. In other words, the actual mobility
process is less favorable for both.

Let us additionally consider the relationship between the
socio-occupational positions held by a given individual at various points in his career. The questionnaire used in the Łódź
studies queried respondents not only about occupation at the
time of first and most recent jobs but also about occupations
at other points in time, i.e., in the years 1946, 1950, 1955, and
1960. The matrix of correlations between positions held in
those years is given in Table 4.

This table includes the whole sample without dividing it into
cohorts. It is evident, however, that the first row of this table
includes only persons beginning work in or before 1946. On the
basis of these data we can measure how much the predictive
power of the initial position weakens with the passage of years.
While the correlation for 1950 is decidedly high (r = 0.788),
for the year 1965 it is much weaker (r = 0.597). Such an attrition of predictive power occurs steadily through the years 1955

Table 4

Correlation Coefficients between Socio-occupational
Positions at Various Points in Time

Years	Years			
	1950	1955	1960	1965
1946	0.788	0.653	0.609	0.597
1950		0.806	0.729	0.725
1955			0.848	0.842
1960				0.920

(r = 0.653) and 1960 (r = 0.609).

The remaining data apply not only to persons who began work in the year indicated in the first column of the table but also to those who had worked previously. Stronger relations can be observed among positions held in the later years of the occupational career. The highest correlation is between the last two points in time, 1960 and 1965. This coefficient is nearly 0.920, which means that over 80% of the variance in 1965 position can be explained by 1960 position.

It is worth mentioning another matter at this point. When we compare the magnitudes of correlation coefficients on the diagonals, we see that these values increase regularly with the passage of time. This suggests that socio-occupational mobility becomes systematically smaller. This hypothesis is also confirmed by examining a variable such as duration of employment. In individual cohorts the values of the correlation coefficients between initial position and position held approximately five years later appear as follows:

    cohort I: 0.780
    cohort II: 0.806
    cohort III: 0.830
    cohort IV: 0.847

In order to interpret this relationship, we must refer to three sets of variables. The first set contains variables concerned with transformations of the socio-occupational structure. It appears that these transformations were stronger at the beginning of the postwar reconstruction and industrialization of the

112

country. This period provided greater opportunities for changing jobs and occupations than existed in later years. Moreover, we should add that toward the end of the fifties the influx of rural population had substantially diminished.[10]

The second set of variables has to do with changes in employment policy. We can expect that policy changes would be in a direction that would produce an ever greater degree of correspondence between the jobs and the incumbents' qualifications. In view of the relatively small number of respondents increasing their educational levels during their occupational careers,[11] this policy can be regarded as a stabilizing influence on the socio-occupational structure.

Finally, as a third set of variables we can list factors of a psychological nature. As a result of the transformations taking place in the socio-occupational structure, the positions held by the respondents in the initial stages of their careers are to an increasing extent positively evaluated by them. Because of this satisfaction there is less need to change the place of work or occupation. Only specific studies, however, could supply the necessary evidence to allow us to determine whether such an explanation is justified.

The Role of Education in the Process of Intragenerational Mobility

It has been shown by many studies conducted in various countries that to a large extent level of education determines socio-occupational position. In particular these studies have shown the influence of education on the progress of the occupational career, where education is measured before the first job, and career is defined as first and most recent occupation.[12] We will begin this part of the paper with a similar problem.

Here we will adopt that model of social mobility in which the education possessed by the respondent just before undertaking first employment (W) determines his socio-occupational position during first employment (P), and both these variables affect, at least somewhat independently of each other, the present position (O). We will explain which of the independent variables (W, P) is more closely related to the dependent variable (O). The data for this analysis are given in Table 5.

Let us look at the values of the zero-order correlation coefficients. All the values are rather high, and using them we can explain 34.4% to 70.8% of the variance in present position. In the first cohort present position is more strongly correlated with education, but in the next three cohorts it is more closely related to initial occupational position. In individual cohorts, however, the differences between the coefficients r_{op} and r_{ow} are not statistically significant.

The zero-order correlations in our analysis contain two com-

Table 5

Correlation Analysis: Present Socio-occupational Position (O)
with Socio-occupational Position at First Employment (P)
and Education Prior to First Employment (W)*

Items	Period of beginning first employment			
measured	before 1946	1946-50	1951-55	1956-60
Multiple correlation R_{opw}	0.680	0.740	0.808	0.850
a) beta for P	0.353	0.551	0.676	0.725
b) beta for W	0.406	0.249	0.166	0.148
Zero-order correlation r_{op}	0.597	0.719	0.798	0.847
Components:				
a) independent of W	0.353	0.551	0.676	0.725
b) through W	0.244	0.168	0.122	0.122
Zero-order correlation r_{ow}	0.618	0.620	0.661	0.732
Components:				
a) independent of P	0.406	0.249	0.166	0.148
b) through P	0.212	0.371	0.495	0.584

*Education scored according to nearest number of completed grades in school: incomplete elementary — 4; full elementary — 7; basic vocational or incomplete secondary — 9; full secondary — 11; incomplete higher — 13; full higher — 16.

ponents. The first component is that part of education's influence on the present job which is independent of the intervening variable, the first job. We can regard this as a direct causal effect. The second component expresses the influence of education on the present job, which is mediated by the first job and thus represents the indirect effect.

In Table 5 it can easily be seen that in each cohort the total correlation between the two positions (O and P) contains a certain amount of indirect causal effect that is a result of the influence of education on the present job. A correlation of this magnitude, however, indicates that the direct effect of the first job is decidedly greater. This shows that occupational beginnings are quite important for the course of a career. In the total correlation between education prior to first job and present occupational position, the component including the influence of the first job is relatively large, especially among persons who began work after 1946. For these people the direct effect of education diminishes over the years shown in the table. Observation of this fact allows us to conclude that the influence of education on first job increases over time. We will return to this problem later.

In Table 5 it is worth noting that in the first cohort, which has been omitted in our description thus far, the present position is more strongly affected by education than by starting position. This may be caused by the fact that, for many reasons, during the period just after the war a considerable number of persons took jobs that did not match their qualifications. This state of affairs could have been a factor in causing individual displacements in the socio-occupational structure such that in the future greater balance could be achieved between the kind of work performed and the level of education at the threshold of the occupational career. On the basis of the data in Table 6, we can see that it is, in fact, education which is more highly correlated with present position than with starting position. This confirms the hypothesis that processes of socio-occupational mobility can contribute to the convergence of at least these two characteristics of social position.[13]

Table 6

Relationship between Education and Socio-occupational Status at Selected Points in Work History

Items measured	Time of beginning initial employment			
	before 1946	1946-50	1951-55	1956-60
Arithmetic mean of school grades completed before engaging in first employment ($\overline{W}$)	7.2	7.3	8.6	8.8
Arithmetic mean of school grades completed at time of last employment ($\overline{Z}$)	7.7	7.9	8.7	8.9
Difference ($\overline{Z} - \overline{W}$)	0.5	0.6	0.1	0.1
Percentage who increased their educational levels during career	10.7	12.2	5.7	4.3
Correlation between education before first employment and socio-occupational status during first employment (r_{pw})	0.598	0.677	0.732	0.806
Correlation between education before first employment and present socio-occupational status (row)	0.618	0.620	0.661	0.732
Correlation between current education and current socio-occupational status (r_{oz})	0.705	0.701	0.735	0.808
Difference ($r_{ow} - r_{pw}$)	+0.020	-0.057	-0.071	-0.074
Difference ($r_{oz} - r_{pw}$)	+0.107	+0.024	+0.002	+0.002

Education and Intragenerational Mobility

The average level of education at the beginning of a career is higher for the younger cohorts. In successive cohorts the arithmetic means of completed school grade were 7.2, 7.3, 8.6, and 8.8. A large jump, 1.3 grades, took place after 1950. Because members of the older cohorts have more frequently completed their education, they differ less than the rest in terms of present education, although they are still behind by almost a whole school year. It must be stressed that the percentages of persons finishing their educations are not much higher than 10% in any cohort, nor are increments of education higher than half a school grade.

The later a cohort began work, the stronger the correlation between education before taking a first job and socio-occupational position at the time of the first job. The same type of rule, though less pronounced, also occurs in the case of analogous variables characterizing an individual at the time of the study. In general, however, we can say that we are witnessing a trend toward an increasing convergence of education and occupation. This trend is the result of complex processes concerned both with the preparation of the labor force and with technical and economic progress.[14]

Relatively comparable data from such countries as the United States, Australia, and the Federal Republic of Germany indicate that among men under 35, the correspondence between the variables of interest here is not higher than in our sample. Data that confirm this statement have been collected and are presented in Table 7.

Although these data do not permit far-reaching conclusions, they suggest the hypothesis that in Poland education plays a more important role in people's occupational careers than it does in capitalist countries. This hypothesis is based on a partially proven assumption that the correlation between inherited status (i.e., father's occupation) and son's education is distinctly weaker in our system. In any event this type of relationship was observed in the neighboring socialist country of Czechoslovakia.[15]

Let us now go on to answer the final but rather basic ques-

117

Table 7

Relationship between Education and Socio-occupational Status
among Men 21-35 in Various Countries

Items measured	USA*	Australia[†]	Germany[‡]	Poland[§]
Education of respondent before engaging in first employment versus socio-occupational status at first employment	n.a.	n.a.	0.86	0.87
Highest level of education of respondent versus socio-occupational status at first employment	0.57	0.41	0.76	0.76
Highest level of education of respondent versus present socio-occupational status	0.66	0.50	0.78	0.79

*Nationwide sample, respondents 25-34; compare P. Blau and O. Duncan, The American Occupational Structure (New York, 1967), p. 178.

[†]General sample, respondents 21-35; compare F. Lancaster Jones, The Process of Stratification in Australia, Seventh World Congress of Sociology, Varna, 1970.

[‡]Sample in the town of Konstanz, respondents 33; compare W. Muller, The Effect of Education before and during Work-Life in Occupational Career, International Workshop on Career Mobility, Konstanz, 1971.

[§]Data for Łódź, respondents 25-35.

tion. This is the issue of whether increasing the educational level after entering the labor force results in any significant movement of individuals among groups in a hierarchy. The answer to this question is based on a comparison of the occupational careers of a subsample of "educationally mobile" respondents with the rest of the population studied.

Among this select group 42.4% more persons experienced socio-occupational advancement than among those who did not change their educational level. This is a very large difference, and it permits us to conclude that people who are "education-

Education and Intragenerational Mobility

ally mobile" also have greater opportunities than the rest of
the population for moving upward in the socio-occupational
hierarchy.

Table 8

Relationship between "Educational Mobility" and
Changes in Socio-occupational Status

	Persons whose current position is			
Educational mobility	higher	the same	lower	N = 100%
Persons who increased their education since starting work	70.0	25.0	5.0	100
Persons who did not increase their education since starting work	27.6	56.6	15.8	892

For the 100 persons who increased their educational level,
we have calculated the correlation coefficient between the number of school grades completed after entering the labor force
and the difference between scores of present and initial positions. The correlation between these variables, which characterizes the degree of mobility, is high — r = 0.689. Therefore
the more individuals increased their levels of education, the
more they advanced in the occupational structure. This is a
statement on the magnitude of the relationship between education and improvement of job position. It strengthens the statement made earlier concerning the existence of the relationship
between these two variables.

Another result worth mentioning is based on a more qualitative analysis. Here we are concerned with those cases in which
increased education did not result in advancement but rather
in occupational stability. In all there were only 25 such cases,
but in several of them (7) we have an interesting disparity between the type of first job and the qualification level. For example, in this category there are some office workers with incomplete elementary education or technicians with incomplete
secondary schooling. We can suppose that in these cases im-

proving their education levels protected them against losing their jobs.

In the future it would be worth testing the hypothesis concerning the existence of two roles which "educational mobility" plays in changing socio-occupational positions, i.e., enhancing upward mobility and preventing downward mobility. In order to show how education influences mobility during different historical periods we would need more extensive data.

Notes

1. Compare with, e.g., P. Blau and O. D. Duncan, The American Occupational Structure (New York, 1967). Since the publication of this paper, several studies have been conducted which have attempted to explain the determining factors in socio-occupational position by means of identical or similar analytic methods. Some of these papers are cited in a later part of this article.

2. Compare R. M. Hauser, "Educational Stratification in the United States," Sociological Inquiry (1970); P. Blau and O. D. Duncan, "Some Preliminary Findings on Social Stratification in the United States," Acta Sociologica 1-2 (1965); W. Muller, "The Effect of Education before and during Work-Life on the Occupational Career," International Workshop on Career Mobility, Konstanz, 1971.

3. Male family heads 21-65 years old were studied. Questionnaire interviews were conducted among 1,000 persons making up a representative sample. Information on the subject is contained in the article by K. M. Słomczyński and W. Wesołowski, "Próby reprezentacyjne i kategorie społeczno-zawodowe," in Zróżnicowanie społeczne, edited by W. Wesołowski (Wrocław: Ossolineum, 1970).

4. On this subject, see K. M. Słomczyński, Zróżnicowanie społeczno-zawodowe i jego korelaty (Wrocław: Ossolineum, 1972).

5. This hierarchy is discussed in greater detail in the book cited in note 4.

6. By the same token this implies that within the framework of specific socio-occupational groups, all persons assume the same position. This position is assumed to be the mean for the whole group.

7. O. D. Duncan, "Methodological Issues in the Analysis of Social Mobility," in N. J. Smelser and S. M. Lipset, eds., Social Structure and Mobility in Economic Development (Chicago, 1966).

8. Analysis of this kind will be presented in a separate article.

9. O. D. Duncan, op. cit.

10. K. Dejmanowska-Janicka, "Społeczne aspekty ruchliwości geograficznej," in Zróżnicowanie społeczne.

11. Compare with later parts of this article.

12. W. Muller, op. cit.

13. This of course does not preclude the fact that socio-occupational mobility can cause other status inconsistencies. Compare K. M. Słomczyński, op. cit.

14. H. Król, Postęp techniczny a kwalifikacje (Warsaw, 1970).

15. Z. Safar, "Basic Data on Social Differentiation in the Czechoslovak Socialist Society," World Congress of Sociology, Varna, 1970.

PART THREE

Class Consciousness and Class Interests

Jan Malanowski

RELATIONS BETWEEN CLASSES AND PERCEPTION OF SOCIAL CLASS DISTANCE*

Introduction

Contemporary Polish sociologists are interested in people's class identification. A number of books and articles have focused on specific classes and social strata. An extensive series of publications edited by J. Szczepański is devoted to the working class and the intelligentsia. A number of other volumes deal with the working class. Studies have been done on the intelligentsia and white-collar workers, as well as farm owners and the special stratum of farmer-workers.[1] Fewest in number are the papers devoted to the propertied classes (with the exception of farmers), that is, to the petite bourgeoisie, landowners, and bourgeoisie who are in the process of adapting to new economic and social conditions.

The literature mentioned above has one common feature: all of it deals with a single social class without considering its place in the structure of society as a whole and without analyzing interclass relations and interdependencies. We have decided to bridge this gap, at least in some small measure, in our own studies. The present paper deals with classes, class

*From Jan Malanowski, Stosunki klasowe i różnice społeczne w mieście (Warsaw: Panstwowe Wydawnictwo Naukowe, 1967), pp. 9-11, 19, 254-65, and 297-302. Abridgements and minor changes have been introduced by the editors with the author's permission.

relations, and social differences in a single town.

Basic information on problems of interest to us was provided by a study of a random sample of the adult population (18 years old and over) made in 1965. In the process we obtained 931 interviews conducted with a questionnaire containing over one hundred questions. A list of voters in the Seym and national elections (May 1965) was used to select the sample because it was the most up-to-date roster of all adult inhabitants of the town.

Opinions on the Existence of Classes

In reflecting on the definition of social class, social theorists often consider the problem of class consciousness. This problem is of particular interest to Marxist sociologists. Apart from theoretical considerations, the problem contains practical aspects. The Marxist definition of class is primarily concerned with the objective criteria of social affiliation. From this theoretical perspective only man's relationship to the means of production, his place in the division of labor, and the degree to which he shares in the national income are important in defining his class position. It is not significant whether a group of people thus defined has a sense of common interest and social solidarity. On the other hand, the theory of class conflict and the concept of political parties (either as representatives of classes or as institutions stimulating awareness of class identity) ascribe great importance to class consciousness.

Social classes can be defined using either objective or subjective criteria, or by using both criteria. It is the end the definition serves and the role it plays in the theory that are important. The sizes of the groups will vary depending on the choice of a definition. If we assume that an important feature of every social class is the awareness of belonging to it and subsequently find that some group does not possess this class awareness, we would conclude that such a group does not constitute a class.

Perception of Class Distance

Furthermore, if we assume that classes are differentiated
by their relationships to the means of production and then find
that such differentiation no longer exists, we would conclude
that classes, defined in this way, have also ceased to exist. If
we draw on other definitional criteria, however, we can study
specific attributes of larger aggregates and ascertain what role
they play in people's lives.

In terms of social class consciousness we were interested in
three factors: opinions on the existence, or lack, of social
classes in contemporary Poland; the number and kinds of existing classes; and self-identification with a given class.

In undertaking a study of this problem, we were aware that
respondents' answers would not be uniform. We first assumed
that the term "social class" would be interpreted by the town's
inhabitants in various ways depending on the level and type of
their education, on individual political viewpoints, or perhaps
on a general level of knowledge. We also assumed that every
adult would have been exposed to this term and used it in everyday speech at some time.

Table 1 shows that a majority of the town's population (52.1%)
expressed the view that social classes do currently exist in

Table 1

"Do you think social classes exist in Poland now?"
Responses (in %)

Social class	Total		Yes	No	Do not know	Missing data
	Number	%				
Total	931	100	52.1	38.6	8.5	0.8
Unskilled workers	234	100	52.1	36.3	10.7	0.9
Skilled workers	193	100	49.7	38.9	10.9	0.5
All blue-collar workers	427	100	51.0	37.5	10.8	0.7
White-collar workers and intelligentsia	307	100	60.2	36.5	2.3	1.0
Petite bourgeoisie	116	100	50.0	40.5	8.6	0.9
Farmers	81	100	29.6	50.6	19.8	—

Source: Sample Survey

127

Jan Malanowski

Poland, 38.6% of the respondents were of the opposite opinion, 8.5% did not know, and missing data accounted for 0.8% of the responses.

Detailed analysis shows a considerable disparity of opinion between representatives of different social strata. White-collar workers (60.2%) and blue-collar workers (51.0%) believed more often than other groups that a class structure exists. A comparable percentage of those believing in the existence of classes was found in the petit bourgeois category (50.0%). The opinions of farm owners, however, were quite astonishing. Only 29.6% of them believed that social classes still exist in Poland. It is somewhat difficult to explain this fact. Perhaps even when farm owners reside in towns, their basic criterion for categorizing people is the town-country distinction. One might also explain this phenomenon by the supposition that the social experience of rural people is so limited that they fail to perceive the complex contemporary urban structure. Two other hypotheses of differing degrees of plausibility can be advanced. The first is that farmers are acquainted with the ideology of the new system to a higher degree than all the remaining social classes; and second, that fearing to voice their own opinions, they have adopted the official stand.

The group of people who expressed a conviction about the classless nature of our society constituted 38.6% of the total respondents, or more than one third. Over half the farmers, 50.6% to be exact, felt that there are no classes in contemporary Poland. In second place was the petite bourgeoisie (40.5%). Blue-collar and white-collar workers expressed a similar opinion (37.5% and 36.5% of their totals), so that there was almost no difference between them.

In conducting the survey we were also interested in how the respondents would justify their opinions that classes do not exist. Of the persons who believed in the classless society, 314 tried to explain their views. We did not perform a quantitative analysis on the content of their responses. We will present the most frequently cited explanations and give examples of the rationale for the answers. We have abstracted 200 of the ques-

tionnaires, or two thirds of the total responses. Among them
153 stated succinctly that equality now exists, and as a result
there can be no classes. All these opinions were expressed in
a single sentence. These were the most frequently encountered
explanations in this group of answers. A woman in her thirties
who is a quality control inspector: "Now everyone is equal."
A woman over 60: "There are no classes because everybody
is equal." A large proportion of the responses connected the
absence of classes with the character of the state, holding that
under socialism there are no classes at all and that exploitation
has been abolished.

In a second group (41 responses) we found a more complicated
justification for the belief that classes do not exist in Poland.
A watch repairman in his thirties explained his opinion in this
way: "Right now everything depends on a person's individual
traits, his capacities, and his diligence." Several people explained that social equality exists because the road to education
is open to all. A woman in her forties, wife of a blue-collar
worker: "Everyone is treated in the same way. At most, some
people earn more, others less." A man in his fifties, a cement
layer by trade: "Everyone has the chance to have a normal,
worthwhile life. The fact that anyone can be educated and that
all have the same rights makes it possible for social classes
to disappear." Both in the first and in the second group of explanations there was a universal belief that the disappearance
of classes is related to the new system of government that has
done away with "landlords" and has eliminated the "exploitation
of the people." This government has introduced "equal treatment of all citizens" and has endowed them with equal rights;
and in addition, it has created identical "starting positions" in
life for all.

Those people who took the position that our society is classless can be identified with groups that are under the influence
of Marxist ideology. Almost 100% of the explanations given for
their opinions bear a close relationship to the materialist theory of socialist society. People who believe that classes do not
exist in Poland, including those not having an opinion, consti-

tute 47.10% of the town's total adult population. This is nearly
one half of the community. Several conclusions emerge from
this fact. First of all, one might suppose that the objective social differences between people are only noticed to a small extent, or that they are treated as natural and equitable. Second,
one could argue that such a community is made up of members
who represent the new society. The question then arises: Why
is it represented most of all by the agrarian and bourgeois
groups? Finally, one could assume that people do not think of
society in terms of class structure but divide it in some different way. This last supposition seems the least likely because
among people who think that social classes still exist there are
(as explained below) a number who divide society according to
their own criteria, which have nothing to do with class divisions.

Perceptions of Social Structure

Here we shall be exclusively concerned with that part of the
population (485 persons, or 52.1% of the respondents) who hold
the opinion that social classes exist in present-day Poland.
From the materialist perspective it is irrelevant whether people are aware of the existence of social classes. Awareness
becomes significant only when we assume that a constitutive
element of social class is the presence of class consciousness.
Thus for the author the study of this question represents neither
evidence nor counterevidence for the existence of classes. In
conducting this study we merely tried to determine the magnitude of differences manifested in the opinions of representatives of specific classes and strata. Moreover, we wanted to
determine how people's perceptions of larger human aggregates
that are neither national nor local are affected by their social
identity. We were also interested in criteria that are used in
dividing people into classes.

In the course of the survey we found that four basic conceptions of social structure occurred most frequently: division
based on realtionship to the means of production; on affluence;

on the degree of access to power; and a class division differentiating the working class, artisans and merchants, farmers, and
the white-collar stratum. The last view, held by 7.6% of the
respondents, asserts the existence of classes, but differentiates
them on the basis of a number of other criteria.

The most frequently mentioned division of society into classes
is, with certain modifications, based on the relationship to the
means of production. Using this criterion the following social
classes emerge: blue-collar workers, white-collar workers,
farmers, and the petite bourgeoisie. Not all those who used
this criterion, however, referred to all of these classes; most
often they talked of one or two of them, forgetting about the
others. Most people remembered the working class (69.8% of
those saying that classes exist), while the petite bourgeoisie
was referred to least frequently. After the working class the
next most frequently mentioned classes in this scheme were
white-collar workers (64.5%) and farmers (52.1%).

We observe appreciable differences between representatives
of different classes in their view of what constitutes the criteria
of class division. Although it is true that the most frequently
encountered criterion was relationship to the means of production, the differences in percent terms are still significant. For
example, 55.6% of the unskilled workers, compared to 81.2% of
the skilled workers, stated that a working class exists. The
petite bourgeoisie and farmers remembered the existence of
blue-collar workers much less frequently (65.5% for the petite
bourgeoisie, 62.5% for farmers) than did white-collar workers
(75.1%).

Among unskilled workers and the petite bourgeoisie who ac-
knowledged the existence of classes, those who used criteria
other than relationship to means of production represented the
largest single category. Close to 43% of unskilled workers and
42.3% of the petite bourgeoisie viewed society as an aggregate
differentiated by either level of affluence or degree of access
to power, or they based the division on still other criteria.
Twenty-five percent of the farmers and 19.7% of the unskilled
laborers expressed the opinion that society consists of the af-

131

fluent class and the poor. This view found fewer supporters among skilled laborers (10.4%) and white-collar workers (13.0%).

One of every ten unskilled workers and even a larger proportion of the petite bourgeoisie (13.8%) thought that society is divided into two classes distinguished by their relationship to power. In the first they included all persons with authority, that is, the ruling class in general. In the second they placed all those who are ruled. Characteristically there were no representatives of this viewpoint among the farmers, only 6.5% among white-collar workers, and 4.2% among skilled workers. The similarity between unskilled workers and the petite bourgeoisie in their perceptions of the social structure is even more surprising, since the views of unskilled workers differed greatly from those of skilled workers. Most interesting, however, are the criteria of class distinction that were relevant to people. It turns out that there are many such criteria. In addition to those mentioned, we find such characteristics as education, occupation, social origin (nobility versus all others), place of residence (urban versus rural), party membership, and religious affiliation, all of which are taken as indicators of class membership.

Social Class Identification

Human attributes such as sex or national identity are unequivocal, and the objective state almost always corresponds to the individual's subjective perception of it. It is a different matter with class membership. Sometimes it happens that persons who would be placed in a given class according to objective criteria do not have a sense of belonging to it. Many different factors are responsible for this discrepancy, but two in particular stand out: peoples' lack of social self-awareness and processes of social mobility. Nor are ambitions and aspirations without effect. A blue-collar worker of farm origin cannot always uniquely specify to what class he belongs. The same is true of people who experience social advancement, and

who in the course of their careers may move up the social ladder several times. The situation is also complicated when we
define the social status of a nonworking spouse by the status of
the working partner. For example, nonworking wives may define their status not on the basis of their husbands' status but
on that of their parents. Keeping these remarks in mind, we go
on to the problem of special interest to us.

Congruence between class identification and objective membership was highest among skilled workers (63.6%) and lowest
among the petite bourgeoisie (18.1%). Let us take a closer look
at self-identification in specific groups and social strata. We
have no data for 6.8% of the unskilled workers, and a number
of them were unable to specify their social status at all.[2]
Nearly 59% considered themselves members of the working
class, and 29.4% identified with other groups and social classes.
Among them the largest group (14.3%) described themselves
using the term "poor people," and only 1.5% claimed to belong
to the group of the moderately affluent. Thus in total, 15.8%
of the members of this stratum described their status using
the criterion of material position.[3] The question on social status was open-ended, so that answers were spontaneous. None
of the unskilled laborers identified himself with the affluent or
the petite bourgeoisie. However, a few (three persons) identified themselves as white-collar workers or intelligentsia, several as farmers, and 4.5% defined their affiliation in terms of
the ruler-ruled distinction.

Skilled workers evaluated their social identity in a different
way than did the unskilled laborers. While 63.6% considered
themselves to be working class, the percentage of those unable
to specify their class membership was only about half as large
as that in the unskilled group. A much larger percentage described themselves as "poor people." Paranthetically, we
should note that in comparison with others, the smallest percentage of those identifying themselves as "poor" occurred in
the skilled labor group (5.3% in the white-collar group, 6.9%
in the petite bourgeoisie, 8.8% of the farmers). Another 5.4%
identified with the farmer or farmer-worker class, and 6.3%

Table 2

"To what social class would you say you belong?"
Social Class Identification (in %)

Social class	Total Number	Total %	Blue-collar workers	Petite bourgeoisie	White-collar workers	Intelligentsia	Farmers	Farmer-workers	Other	Missing data
Total	556	100	42.1	3.2	5.0	15.5	5.2	0.5	23.6	4.9
Unskilled workers	133	100	58.5	–	0.8	1.5	3.0	–	29.4	6.8
Skilled workers	110	100	63.6	1.8	2.7	3.6	4.5	0.9	15.6	7.3
All blue-collar workers	243	100	60.9	0.8	1.6	2.5	3.7	0.4	23.1	7.0
White-collar workers and intelligentsia	207	100	24.2	1.4	10.6	37.2	1.9	0.5	20.3	3.9
Petite bourgeoisie	72	100	43.1	18.1	1.4	2.8	2.8	–	29.0	2.8
Farmers	34	100	14.7	–	2.9	2.9	41.2	2.9	35.4	–

Source: Sample Survey

134

with the white-collar group. Twice as many (3.6%) skilled as unskilled workers identified with the moderately affluent group, and 1.8% with the petite bourgeoisie.

In the stratum of white-collar workers, a small percentage (1.4%) could not define their social identity, and data are lacking for 3.9%. Another 47.8% considered themselves white-collar workers and intelligentsia, and of them, 37.2% specified intelligentsia, and only 10.6% said white-collar workers. A sizable percentage (24.2%) of white-collar workers reported association with the working class. Several reasons probably account for this. The most important, however, is the desire to emphasize a generic relationship to men of labor. Moreover, 2.4% of the white-collar group identified with farmers and farmer-workers, and 10.1% defined their social standing in terms of material status, with 5.3% considering themselves "poor" and 4.8% "affluent" or "moderately affluent."

As we mentioned above, the lowest degree of agreement between objective class membership and its subjective assessment was found among the petite bourgeoisie. In this class only 18.1% identified themselves as petite bourgeoisie, while 43.1% identified with the working class. The fact that such a large percentage of artisans and persons connected to them by family ties had a sense of belonging to the working class is noteworthy. The basis for this is in the material condition and type of work performed by the artisan group. Not one merchant was found in the sample (the number of merchants in the town's area is so small that they could easily not have found their way into the town's 10% sample). The petite bourgeoisie in our sample were almost exclusively artisans. The small-town artisan, while differing objectively in many respects from the worker (having his own means of production and source of income), nonetheless has a sense of common identity with workers as men of labor. The artisans belonged to both the PPS (Polish Socialist Party) and KPP (Communist Party of Poland). After the war the artisans made up about one fourth of the total PPR (Polish Workers' Party) membership. Petty artisans, like workers, suffered as much from dire poverty and exploitation as from unemployment. Almost 7% of the artisans did not know how to define their social identity, and 9.7% used the material status criterion. Of all the groups the petite bourgeoisie were most likely (1.4%) to see themselves as affluent; no farmers or laborers said this. A small percentage, however, claimed affiliation with farmers (2.8%) and with white-collar workers (4.2%).

In the farmer class 44.1% considered themselves farmers, and of them, 2.9% described themselves as farmer-workers. Another 14.7% considered themselves blue-collar workers, and 11.8% did not know where to place themselves socially. Among the farmers 14.7% differentiated society using material status. Of them, 5.9% considered themselves "moderately affluent," and 8.8% "poor." None of the farmers thought that society is divided into the "ruling class" and the "ruled."

Evaluations of Interclass Relations

We posed a series of ten questions to all respondents in order to obtain their opinions about the character of interclass relations. We wanted to determine how the various classes coexist within the town. There were three evaluations of their relationships: "they live in harmony with each other"; "they are indifferent to each other"; and "they dislike each other."

On the basis of the responses, we are able to describe interclass relations as perceived by representatives of various classes. We assumed that we could divide the members of each class into three groups depending on their opinions. Those who think that social harmony exists between classes make up the first group. The second group is composed of people who believe that interclass antagonisms exist. The third contains those who describe class relations with the phrase "they are indifferent to each other." This indicates a lack of social harmony as much as the absence of conflict. Such people think that one class is unnoticed by another, that nothing unites them, but neither does anything divide them. The size of these groups changes depending on which particular class is considered.

Perception of Class Distance

We will begin our discussion by presenting the opinions of blue-collar workers concerning the relations binding them with other social classes and social strata. Animosity between blue- and white-collar workers is not a universal phenomenon, although a large proportion of blue-collar workers perceived it. The phrase "They dislike each other" can be interpreted in two ways: either lightly or more strictly, as describing antagonism. Typical of all such responses is their relationship to perceptions of social distance and thus the acknowledgment of essential disparities and sources of conflict between people. In the blue-collar group 31.1% of the workers thought that white- and blue-collar workers "dislike each other," and 39.6% thought that they "live in harmony." Although more were convinced of harmony than the opposite, we cannot underestimate the problem. In any case, white-collar workers also affirmed the existence of conflict, though to a slightly lesser degree (27%) than the blue-collar workers. The petite bourgeoisie perceived the existence of conflict between blue- and white-collar workers to a greater extent (33.6%) than did farmers (19.8%). The worker-intelligentsia tension was most keenly felt by the workers, since a larger percentage of them were convinced of its existence. The most harmonious relations seemed to exist between the workers and the artisans. Roughly one out of every ten workers voiced the opinion that artisans and manual laborers dislike each other; the artisans expressed this opinion about as often (10.3%). The antagonism between workers and merchants was twice as strong. In this case one in every five workers (21.3%) observed the existence of animosity between merchants and workers. While 55% of the total responding workers were of the opinion that they live in harmony with artisans, the corresponding percentage in the case of merchants was only 32.1%, or 23% lower. We also found a small degree of animosity between farmers and blue-collar workers.

Among the workers 7.5% thought that enmity and prejudice exist between themselves and farmers. Farmers similarly noted the unfavorable attitude of workers (6.2%). Among the workers 69.1% held the opinion that their relations with farmers

137

Jan Malanowski

are harmonious, but only 46.9% of the farmers believed this.
The information obtained on the mutual assessment of contacts
between farmers and workers departed considerably from popular beliefs, and also from the results of certain studies.[4] We
should note first of all that economic conflicts do exist between
blue-collar workers and farmers. They arise from competition
in the labor market and from differences in the standard of living. It would seem, then, that the workers should take a more
skeptical view of the farmers, but the results show the opposite.

To summarize, in looking at the class relations between
workers and other groups we have found the following: blue-
collar workers expressed the greatest mistrust of white-collar
workers, whereas the least amount of discord occurred between
blue-collar workers, artisans, and farmers. A marked predominance of positive evaluations characterizes the relations
between workers and other classes. Therefore the prevailing
character of the worker's attitude to other classes is either
accord or indifference. The workers assessed their relations
with artisans and farmers most favorably.

Let us now look at judgments on the interclass relations of
white-collar workers. White-collar workers assessed their
relations with the petite bourgeoisie most favorably. Among
the respondents 51.2% considered them harmonious, and only
11.4% believed that enmity and prejudice exist between white-
collar workers and artisans.

Merchants appear to be a sector of the petite bourgeoisie
with which white-collar workers are not in conflict. Only 12.1%
of the respondents maintained that white-collar workers "dislike" merchants. Representatives of other classes were even
less likely to believe this: to wit, only 2.5% of the farmers observed such conflicts, and 7% of the blue-collar workers. Perceptions of harmonious relations were even more common between white-collar workers and artisans. Thus both blue-collar
workers and farmers saw little animosity between these two
social strata. White-collar workers saw the greatest amount
of tension in their relations with blue-collar workers and farmers; 27.4% of the respondents believed that animosity exists
with farmers; and likewise 27.9% with blue-collar workers.

138

Perception of Class Distance

Half as many farmers reported enmity and lack of empathy between themselves and blue-collar workers as with the white-collar workers, more than one third could not assess those relations, and only 29.7% were convinced that they are harmonious. An overwhelming majority of white-collar workers described their relations with other classes and social strata as harmonious or indifferent, just as blue-collar workers did.

The petite bourgeoisie and the farmers indicated that they have the best relations with other classes. In their eyes there is no serious social friction between them and other classes. Farmers had the largest percentage admitting to a dislike of white-collar workers (13.6%). White-collar workers aroused the strongest feelings of social antagonism among the farmers. Blue-collar workers aroused such feeling in 6.2% of the farmers, merchants in 11.1%, and artisans in 2.5%. The greatest harmony and good feeling existed between artisans and farmers.

We should add paranthetically that farmers had the most difficulty answering questions concerning their assessment of inter-class relations within the town. Twenty-seven percent of them could not answer at least once, and 11.1% of the farmers voiced the belief that relations between classes are based on harmony. It seems that farmers are the group with the least developed sense of social isolation, and also with the least developed knowledge of society. The fact that more than a fourth did not know how to answer questions concerning the relation of their class to other classes seems to support the validity of such a hypothesis.

The petite bourgeoisie also felt that their relationships with other classes were only slightly antagonistic, if at all. In the consciousness of the petite bourgeoisie, however, the amount of conflict between artisans and other classes was perceived as different from the amount of conflict arising from the relationship of merchants to other classes. The petite bourgeoisie themselves believed that there is a deeper conflict between merchants and the rest of the urban community than between artisans and the rest of the community.

The best relations, according to the petite bourgeoisie, prevail between artisans and merchants (i.e., within their own social class) and between farmers and artisans. Only 5.2% of the petite bourgeoisie felt animosity toward farmers, 10.3% of them toward blue-collar workers, and 11.2% toward white-collar workers. The assessment of relations between merchants and the remaining classes, and especially the working class, assumed a more trenchant character.

Summarizing the discussion of interclass relations as reflected in the consciousness of the town's inhabitants, we must conclude that feelings of harmony, lack of conflict, and indifference outweigh mistrust and animosity. Blue- and white-collar workers have the most friction with other social classes; farmers and petite bourgeoisie have the least. We must keep in mind, however, that all this applies to a general assessment of interclass relations.

Notes

1. Editors' note: A farmer-worker is an individual whose principal occupation is on an individual family farm but who also has a nonfarm job.

2. Here we consider only those respondents who answered affirmatively to the question about the existence of social classes. We also include those 71 individuals who answered that there were no social classes, but who identified the class to which they belonged.

3. These responses are included in the category "other" in Table 2.

4. See J. Malanowski, Robotnicy Warszawskiej Fabryki Motocykli (Wrocław: Ossolineum, 1962), p. 94; Maria Jarosinska, Adaptacja młodzieży wiejskiej do klasy robotniczej (Wrocław: Ossolineum, 1964), p. 170.

Krzysztof Szafnicki

EVALUATIONS OF INDIVIDUAL EARNINGS AND FAMILY INCOME*

Introduction

Empirical data concerning objective and subjective dimensions of the social situation of individuals and social groups enable us to clarify the following issues: (1) how individual earnings are distributed and how they are evaluated by respondents, and (2) how family incomes compare with incomes considered adequate by respondents. The choice of these two questions is dictated by the contention that in our society the distribution of earnings is associated with a certain potential for conflict. It is sometimes said that the division of goods violates the general principle of payment according to work performed and as such induces social tensions.[1] Therefore it seems important to discover the factors that affect an individual's assessment of his earnings. It is particularly worth knowing to what extent this assessment is determined by the level of earnings and to what extent it is motivated by other factors, such as type of work, occupation, educational level, and age.

On the other hand, in comparing actual family incomes with

*From Krzysztof Szafnicki, "Oceny płac individualnych i dochódow rodzin," in K. Słomczyński and W. Wesołowski, eds., <u>Struktura i ruchliwość społeczna</u> (Wrocław: Ossolineum, 1973), pp. 33-60. Abridgements and minor editorial changes introduced by the editors with the author's consent.

the incomes considered adequate by respondents, we would like to determine in which social groups the disparity between the real and desired situations is greatest. We would also like to know whether implementation of the desired wage distribution would create "greater equality."

Using material obtained in Szczecin and Koszalin in 1964 and in Łódź in the years 1965 to 1967, we will describe certain patterns in the formation of assessments of individual income and judgments on adequate family income.[2] These questions regarding earnings and incomes were part of a larger survey, but in our opinion this material is extremely valuable because it constitutes a frame of reference for analyzing the present state of social consciousness.

Earnings Level and Evaluations

Respondents were asked: "In your opinion are your earnings appropriate for the occupation (position) in which you work?" They had to choose an answer from one of five points on the scale: (1) they are considerably higher; (2) they are somewhat higher; (3) they are suitable; (4) they are somewhat lower; or (5) they are considerably lower. Table 1 shows the distribution of individual evaluations. As we see, the extent of dissatisfaction (that is, the proportion of persons choosing the last two points on the scale) decreases with an increase in earning level to 3,001-4,000 złotys. The decrease in dissatisfaction is not large, since the percentage of persons with the highest earnings that chose the lowest two points on the scale does not fall below 50% and is only about one quarter less than the proportion with the lowest earnings.

On this basis we might expect a rather prevalent conviction that the wage scale is too low; second, that people's attitudes about earnings are only slightly determined by the wage scale; and third, that people who think their earnings are too low in relation to their occupation and position most often choose an evaluation that is moderately rather than extremely negative.

142

Evaluations of Earnings and Incomes

Table 1

Evaluation of Earnings
(Szczecin, Koszalin, Łódź, 1965)

Gross monthly earnings in złotys	Percentage of persons who think their wages are:			
	much and somewhat too high	suitable	somewhat too low	much too low
Up to 1,000	4.0	16.7	35.5	43.8
1,001-2,000	1.0	20.4	42.3	36.0
2,001-3,000	0.8	35.6	45.1	18.5
3,001-4,000	1.1	47.3	37.4	14.2
4,001-5,000	3.4	39.4	35.9	21.3
5,001 and more	6.5	41.9	35.5	16.1

This suggests the hypothesis that in our society there is a general sense of relative deprivation, although this conviction is not strongly held.

The Effect of Selected Factors
on Positive Assessment of Earnings

First, let us see if people in various occupational categories who earn the same amount are equally satisfied. These results are contained in Table 2. Only in the lowest earnings category are there equal percentages of people across socio-occupational categories who perceive their wages as suitable. We also observe that the percentage of satisfied people with medium and highest earnings is greater among manual workers than among white-collar workers. We can conclude that the effect of the nature of work and qualifications on earnings satisfaction increases with the level of earnings.

We find a similar relationship in analyzing the statements of people with differing levels of education. In general, then, physical work, lower education, and a high pay scale favor the acceptance of the respondent's earnings. In other investigations we have also confirmed that increasing age has an effect in the

Table 2

Effect of Occupation and Level of Earnings
on Evaluation of Wages
(Szczecin, Koszalin, Łódź, 1965)

Socio-occupational categories	Monthly earnings in złotys		
	up to 2,000	2,001-3,000	3,001 and more
	Percentage of persons who think their wages are suitable		
Intelligentsia	6.6	23.5	36.9
Office workers	21.9	37.5	57.4
Technicians	27.2	37.9	51.0
Lower-level white-collar workers	20.2	29.7	61.5
Master craftsmen and foremen	20.6	43.5	70.6
Skilled workers	21.6	42.5	63.3
Semiskilled workers	27.9	33.3	*
Unskilled laborers	20.3	50.0	*

*The percentage was not calculated because of a small numerical base.

same direction. We can now go one step further in determining the effects of each independent variable as well as their total effect on satisfaction.

Multivariate models for dichotomous characteristics developed by J. Coleman[3] are one of the techniques that make it possible to measure the effects of individual variables and their sum. In these models all variables are in one of two possible states: 1, when the given characteristic is present, and 0, when it is not. Since we are interested in an increase in the proportion of people who are satisfied with their earnings, this corresponds to state 1 of our dependent variable. In our models state 1 of the independent variables is:

— age over 45, physical work, earnings over 3,000 złotys per month in the first model;

— age over 45, less than secondary education, earnings over 3,000 złotys in the second model.

Evaluations of Earnings and Incomes

Thus the models with two identical independent characteristics (age and wages) have the same state 1 and differ only with respect to the third independent characteristic (type of work and education).

Using both models we will be in a position to measure how much each individual characteristic affects earnings satisfaction, how much the sets of three characteristics taken together affect it, and to what extent it is influenced by uncontrolled factors, i.e., random fluctuations. The empirical data necessary for calculating components of the effect are contained in Tables 3 and 4. The expected values, constituting a test of the adequacy of these models, are also provided in the tables.

In the first model the strength of the age effect is expressed by the quantity $a_1 = 0.027$; of the type of work by $a_2 = 0.129$; of gross earnings by $a_3 = 0.192$; of random fluctuations in the di-

Table 3

Effect of Age, Type of Work, and Wages
on Positive Assessment of Earnings
(Model 1)

Age	Type of work	Gross wage level in złotys	Observed proportion of persons satisfied with earnings	Expected proportion of persons satisfied with earnings	Difference between observed and expected proportions
Below 45 years	blue-collar worker	up to 3,000	0.279	0.340	−0.061
		3,000 and over	0.461	0.532	−0.071
	white-collar worker	up to 3,000	0.298	0.211	+0.087
		3,000 and over	0.446	0.403	+0.043
Over 45 years	blue-collar worker	up to 3,000	0.329	0.367	−0.038
		3,000 and over	0.727	0.569	+0.158
	white-collar worker	up to 3,000	0.249	0.238	+0.011
		3,000 and over	0.288	0.430	−0.142

Table 4

Effect of Age, Education, and Wages
on Positive Assessment of Earnings
(Model 2)

Age	Education level	Gross wage level in złotys	Observed proportion of persons satisfied with earnings	Expected proportion of persons satisfied with earnings	Difference between observed and expected proportions
Below 45 years	below secondary	up to 3,000	0.194	0.233	−0.039
		3,000 and more	0.410	0.416	−0.006
	secondary and higher	up to 3,000	0.225	0.195	+0.030
		3,000 and more	0.399	0.378	+0.021
Over 45 years	below secondary	up to 3,000	0.261	0.244	+0.017
		3,000 and more	0.456	0.427	+0.029
	secondary and higher	up to 3,000	0.194	0.206	−0.012
		3,000 and more	0.351	0.389	−0.028

rection of greater dissatisfaction, s = 0.441. In the second
model the set of variables expresses the effect of age, represented by the quantity a_1 = 0.011; of education, a_2 = 0.038; of
gross earnings, a_3 = 0.183; of random fluctuations in the direction of greater satisfaction, r = 0.195; of random fluctuations
in the direction of greater dissatisfaction, s = 0.573.

In both models we are struck by the absence of a dominant
factor among the parameters, i.e., one which would have decidedly greater explanatory power than the remaining factors.
Although level of earnings affects the respondents more than
the type of work, the difference is not significant. Apart from
a totally insignificant effect of age and a minimal effect of education, the "significant" variables explain only 35% of the
change in the direction of greater satisfaction.

However, the adequacy test shows that in the first model there

146

are large deviations of certain observed proportions from the
expected values. Among manual workers over 45 and receiving
wages over 3,000 złotys, we find a much higher proportion of
satisfied people than the model had predicted. However, among
white-collar workers over 45 with higher pay, the analogous
proportion is much lower than expected. Among people less
than 45 we note an unexpectedly high percentage of white-collar
workers who are satisfied with their earnings and an unexpectedly low percentage of satisfied manual workers.

The deviations are appreciable, and they indicate that in
reality, in addition to the basic trends included in the model,
there are complementary trends in which the actual pattern of
interaction among the variables does not coincide with the model. Therefore the first model is inadequate to explain the data.
In the second model the deviations are relatively small and
randomly distributed. In this case, however, formal fit is accompanied by an insignificant explanatory value.

Perhaps it would be better to describe the interaction among
the variables by considering only a single model: level of education, type of work, and level of earnings. In our case this
was not possible because of the small population size and a high
correlation of education with level of earnings and type of work.

Younger, more educated blue-collar workers have higher aspirations and, as a result, a more critical attitude toward their
own earnings. On the other hand, a higher level of education is
associated with higher earnings, and higher earnings encourage,
as we have seen, a positive assessment. We would then have a
twofold education effect: through higher aspirations toward negative assessment, and through higher earnings toward an acceptance of existing conditions. Using this approach, individual
satisfaction would be the result of two opposing tendencies.

In order to characterize individuals in terms of the degree
of disparity between aspirations and the realm of possibilities,
we would have to consider not only individual characteristics
but their interaction effects as well. At the same time, we should
not limit ourselves to objective characteristics. K. Słomczyński
has shown that when education and income are held constant,

147

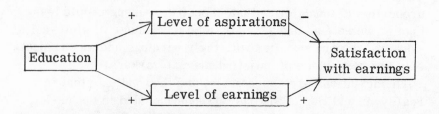

the percentage of persons who are dissatisfied with their earnings increases with respondents' higher assessments of their educational attainment.[4]

The interaction scheme would have the form:

(The + sign indicates a unidirectional positive effect.
The − sign indicates a unidirectional negative effect.)

Actual and Adequate Family Incomes

We shall now consider the respondents' opinions on the financial situation of their families. The materials at our disposal enabled us to determine not only family incomes but also whether in the respondents' opinions these incomes are adequate. After the question on joint monthly incomes of all the family members, respondents were asked: "What total income would you consider adequate for your family?"[5]

The purpose of the question was to discover the level of financial aspirations, and for this reason the respondents were given complete freedom in interpreting the term "adequate income." It seems, however, that by "adequate income" they most often meant one that would be sufficient to fulfill currently felt needs. Starting with this assumption, the difference between the aspiration level and the actual level of income was taken as a measure of the degree of the respondents' dissatisfaction with the financial situation of their families. In this way we consciously avoided the problem of which needs, and to what degree these needs, could be fulfilled with incomes considered

Table 5

Distribution and Mean Level of Actual and Adequate Incomes
per Family Member in Two Cities (in %)

Cities	Income	Income level in złotys								Other responses and missing data	Mean (in złotys)
		up to 400	401-500	501-600	601-800	801-1,000	1,001-1,500	1,501-2,000	2,001 and more		
Szczecin	Actual	7.3	10.3	11.7	19.5	19.2	23.1	5.9	2.1	0.6	885
	Adequate	0.4	2.7	4.6	13.8	20.6	28.1	14.3	7.6	8.1	1,217
Koszalin	Actual	8.9	9.5	8.3	23.3	20.5	21.0	5.7	2.1	0.7	874
	Adequate	0.8	2.5	3.7	15.1	19.7	25.3	14.8	6.8	11.3	1,217

satisfactory. This was necessary because we wanted to concentrate our attention on a specific state of social awareness. We shall determine by how many złotys the level of "adequate" incomes exceeds the level of actual incomes in absolute terms (absolute difference, nonrelative increment), whereas in relative terms we shall determine by how much "adequate" incomes exceed actual incomes (relative difference, relative increment).

In answer to the question on the level of satisfactory family income, approximately 90% of the respondents quoted concrete sums of money.[6] In Table 5 the distribution of these amounts is compared with the distribution of actual income. This comparison suggests three important conclusions:

1. There is a similar structure of actual incomes in both cities. Differences in the percentages of families in particular income brackets do not exceed 4%; this is reflected in roughly equal means.

2. In the case of adequate incomes, the similarity of distributions for both cities is even higher. The differences in percentages do not exceed 3%, and the means are identical.

3. Within each city there is considerable disparity between the distributions and average levels of actual and adequate incomes.

Thus in both cities neither the objective situation nor the opinions of their residents differ to an appreciable extent. This allows us to combine the two urban samples for further analysis. The distribution curves for real and satisfactory incomes, as shown in Figure 1, are for the combined sample, and they answer the question: "What part of the population obtains an income below a certain threshold, and what part considers such an income satisfactory?" From these cumulative graphs we can see that adequate incomes are no smaller than 400 złotys per person, but in actuality 8% of the families are found below this "subjective minimum." In total, almost 50% of the sample families earned incomes below 800 złotys per person, and less than 20% would want to earn that amount. Two percent of the families have incomes above 2,000 złotys per person, and 7% would like to have that amount. Can we then

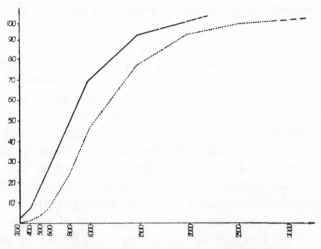

.... adequate income per family member
————— actual income per family member

Figure 1. Distribution curves of actual and adequate incomes.

consider the disparities between adequate and actual incomes
to be large? In order to answer that question we will compare
means. The average level of adequate income exceeds 1,200
złotys, whereas the mean level of actual incomes does not exceed
900 złotys. Although the absolute difference (around 300 złotys)
is not very large, the relative difference (around 33%) is large.

How does the internal differentiation of incomes, i.e., their
dispersion, appear in the objective and subjective dimensions?
The value of the coefficient of variation calculated for actual
incomes (V = 45.3%) is somewhat lower than for the adequate
incomes (V = 47.0%). The difference is not large, which indicates that the attainment of adequate incomes would not produce
a less differentiated population than the one that exists in reality. The postulated increase in the range of incomes and
changes in the proportion of families in the various income cat-
egores would not affect the character of the distribution. This
important conclusion should be tested on a larger sample, since
it indicates that the main thrust of social criticism does not aim at
the degree of differentiation of family incomes but at their level.

151

Krzysztof Szafnicki

Interdependence between the Levels of Actual and Adequate Family Income

Data that show how the objective situation of families is related to the respondent's level of financial aspirations and to the degree of his income dissatisfaction are presented in Table 6.

For each income range we can see the mean level of adequate incomes (column 2), by how many złotys (column 3), and to what degree (column 4) the satisfactory incomes exceed the real financial situations of families. This last item of information is treated as a measure of the level of income dissatisfaction.

In all categories adequate incomes exceed actual. The absolute level of adequate incomes, i.e., the level of aspirations, increases with a rise in actual income. In general the absolute difference between the level of income earned and that desired also increases. Going from absolute to relative differences, we note the reverse trend: higher income implies a relatively

Table 6

Relation between Average Levels
of Actual and Adequate Income

Midpoint of actual income category (in złotys)	Mean adequate income per family respondent (in złotys)	Difference between mean of adequate income and mid-point of actual income category (in złotys)	Relative excess of adequate income over actual income (in % of actual income)
300	540	265	96
350	722	372	107
450	724	274	61
550	835	285	52
700	1,031	331	47
900	1,290	390	43
1,250	1,685	435	35
1,750	2,154	404	23
2,000	2,769	519	23
Total population	1,217	358	42

Evaluations of Earnings and Incomes

lower level of income considered adequate, which means that
ideal incomes exceed actual to an ever decreasing degree. The
general conclusion is that almost all the respondents aspire to
incomes higher than those they have at their disposal and thus
are to some extent dissatisfied with the financial situation of
their families. Dissatisfaction, however, is felt much more
strongly among persons who are in objectively lower circumstances than among persons whose material situation is better.

In the light of this conclusion it is worth looking more closely
at the relationship between the level of actual income and the
aspiration level. In Figure 2 we can see that the mean levels
of adequate incomes increase with a rise in actual incomes in
a fairly regular manner, and this leads us to suspect a linear
relationship between the two. Moreover, the intermediate values fall around a straight line, which indicates the existence of
a strong correlation between both variables.

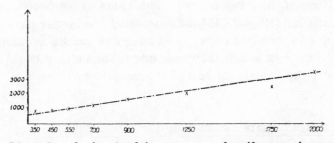

Mean level of actual income per family member.
Figure 2. Relation between the levels of actual and adequate
incomes.

The correlation between real incomes and aspirations turns
out indeed to be quite high (r = 0.793) and is statistically significant. Thus we can predict with a rather high degree of accuracy the level of satisfactory income if the magnitude of actual
income is known, and vice versa. The dependence of aspiration
on income level can be described by the regression equation

$$\overline{Y} = 244 \text{ złotys} + 1.127x,$$

where x denotes the amount of actual income.

153

Knowing the financial aspiration level of the head of the household, we can estimate the level of actual earnings of the family using the equation

$$\overline{X} = 184 \text{ złotys} + 0.557y,$$

where y denotes the size of income considered satisfactory.

Let us compare the mean levels of adequate incomes calculated earlier for a given level of actual incomes with the mean levels estimated on the basis of the first equation. The comparison shows that this equation yields a relatively good estimate of the real level of adequate income. Larger deviations pertain only to persons with incomes somewhat higher than the minimum (adequate incomes are "too high") and to persons with incomes somewhat lower than the maximum (adequate incomes are "too low").

The financial situation of the family thus affects the financial aspirations of the respondents. The value of the coefficient of determination ($R^2 = 0.638$) indicates that the larger part of the difference in incomes considered adequate can be ascribed to the difference in actual incomes, and other factors could explain only the remaining 36% of the variance.

Actual and Adequate Incomes of Socio-occupational Groups and Categories

A comparison of mean levels of actual and adequate incomes of the various socio-occupational groups and categories is contained in Table 7. This comparison leads to a series of generalizations.

Compared to manual workers, white-collar workers have a decidedly higher aspiration level and a decidedly larger absolute difference between actual and adequate incomes. However, among manual workers, despite lower aspirations and a lower absolute difference between actual and adequate income levels, there is a higher degree of satisfaction. The incomes of blue-collar workers are, on the average, over 40% lower than those

Table 7

Socioeconomic Categories by Mean Level of Actual and Adequate Incomes per Family Member (Szczecin, Koszalin)

Socio-occupational categories	Mean of actual incomes per family member (in złotys)	Mean of adequate incomes per family member (in złotys)	Difference between mean values of actual and adequate incomes per family member (in złotys)	Relative excess of mean adequate income over mean actual income (in % of actual income)
Intelligentsia	1,229	1,632	403	33
Technicians	1,019	1,382	363	36
Office workers	951	1,295	344	36
Lower-level white-collar workers	780	1,064	284	36
Master craftsmen and foremen	874	1,152	278	32
Skilled workers	734	1,063	329	45
Unskilled workers	644	947	303	47
White-collar workers (intelligentsia, technicians, and office workers)	1,058	1,434	376	35
Blue-collar workers (skilled, semiskilled, and unskilled)	722	1,033	311	43

considered adequate, whereas the incomes of white-collar workers are around 35% lower. Comparing the incomes of extreme socio-occupational categories (intelligentsia and unskilled laborers), we note that in order to achieve a satisfactory state, it is necessary for the incomes of the former to rise by a third and of the latter by almost half. In addition to the intelligentsia, master craftsmen and foremen seem to be most satisfied with the status quo, being inclined to content themselves with a 32% rise in the financial resources of their families.

Comparing the white-collar and blue-collar groups, we find that the ratios of means are 1.47:1 for actual incomes and 1.39:1 for satisfactory incomes. The attainment of the income level that the groups judge to be "an equitable family income" would imply a simultaneous reduction in differences between these groups. This conclusion is all the more important and interesting in that a decrease of differences between these groups would occur together with a constant degree of intragroup differentiation (the coefficient of variation for actual incomes is V = 42.2% for white-collar workers, V = 44.3% for blue-collar workers, and for adequate incomes, V = 44.0% and 43.7%, respectively) and also, as we saw earlier, with a slight rise in income differentiation for the whole population treated as an aggregate of families.

The above conclusion also applies to narrow socio-occupational categories. The actual ratio of average income of the intelligentsia to that of unskilled workers (around 1.90:1) would decrease slightly (to around 1.70:1) if the wishes of both categories were satisfied, that is, if incomes were divided according to the prescription "To each family according to its financial aspirations."

Summarizing the arguments above, we can say that the incomes of blue-collar workers, especially unskilled workers, depart more than the incomes of other socio-occupational groups and categories from the satisfactory level. At the same time, the existing level of social awareness favors the reduction of intergroup differences, together with the preservation — and even a slight increase — of intragroup differentiation.

156

Evaluations of Earnings and Incomes

Notes

1. A. Sarapata writes: "In a system in which payment according to work performed becomes a constitutional norm expressing the achievement of working men... the realization of a division which is not in accordance with these views and expectations evokes a feeling of injustice and changes a favorable attitude into an unfavorable one." Studia nad uwarstwieniem i ruchliwością społeczna w Polsce (Warsaw, 1965), p. 247. Among others, the following authors have noted the limitations on applying the principle of payment according to work: J. Sztumski Kształtowanie się i funkcjonowanie bodźców ekonomicznych i pozaekonomicznych wpływających na wydajność pracy w przemyśle (Torun, 1966), and L. Borcz, Zasada wynagradzania według pracy w teorii i praktyce przemysłu (Warsaw, 1970).

2. Editors' note: The studies covered working males who were 21-65 years of age and family heads. Questionnaire interviews were conducted with 630 residents of Koszalin, 1,051 residents of Szczecin, and 2,000 residents of Łódź (1,000 in 1965; 1,000 in 1967). Representative samples were selected systematically from the files of urban residents in Koszalin and Szczecin, and in both Łódź surveys, from the voting registers. See K. Słomczyński and W. Wesołowski, "Proby reprezantacyjne i kategorie społeczno-zawodowe," in W. Wesołowski, ed., Zróżnicowanie społeczne (Wrocław: Ossolineum, 1970).

3. J. Coleman, Introduction to Mathematical Sociology (Glencoe, Ill.: Free Press, 1964).

4. K. Słomczyński, Zróżnicowanie społeczno-zawodowe i jego korelaty (Wrocław, 1972), p. 196.

5. Both actual and adequate income were recorded in the form of net income.

6. A number of respondents did not give an amount of satisfactory income (see data in Table 5). We excluded this group from further study.

Jadwiga Koralewicz-Zębik

POWER IN THE VALUE SYSTEMS OF
SELECTED SOCIAL GROUPS*

Overview

The basic problem in this study is the search for similarities and
differences in the value systems of various socio-occupational
categories. This problem has not yet been studied empirically
in Poland; there are no comparative studies on the value systems of different socio-occupational categories within strata
and classes. [1]

The basis for this discussion will be empirical research on
strategically chosen groups — engineers, skilled workers, and
private producers (mainly artisans) in a large city. Each of
these collectivities is situated differently in the class-stratum
structure and represents a different segment of it: intelligentsia, blue-collar workers, and small-scale merchandise producers. The studies took place in Łódź in 1969 and involved a
sample of 200 members of each selected socio-occupational
category. Structured interviews were used to gather the data.

In one study it is not possible to encompass the entire value
systems of these groups or to detect and hierarchically order
all their values. For this reason the researcher is faced with

_____

*From Jadwiga Koralewicz-Zębik, System wartości a struktura
społeczna (Wrocław: Ossolineum, 1974), pp. 10-12, 68-75, 104-6, and
229-42. Abbreviations and minor editorial changes were introduced
by the editors with the author's consent.

158

the necessity of making a choice. Since my research is the result of an interest in social structure, I have chosen to study values concerning incomes, formal education, managerial positions, and cultural consumption. This choice was conditioned by the determinations and results of previous studies on the differentiation of Polish society. Education, income, participation in power, and cultural consumption have proved to be the relevant criteria of social divisions, the factors that define the status of individuals and groups in the class-stratum structure.

Moreover, according to public opinion the differences between people in education, income, participation in power, and cultural consumption constitute the most important obstacles to the elimination of remaining social distances and barriers.[2] Therefore I hypothesized that these attributes should be universally valued.[3]

Method of Study

The interview consisted of two parts. In the first a questionnaire that contained questions with response categories, as well as open-ended questions, was administered. By means of these we hoped to measure both the intrinsic and instrumental scope of each of the four general values. Questions about the value hierarchy were included. We also asked questions about the level or kind of values considered especially attractive within the framework of each of the four general values. The last group of questions concerned the characteristics of the respondent's social position.

In the second part of the interview the respondents read short narratives of conflict situations that involved choosing between levels of two different values. One of the main objectives of using these short narratives was to determine the hierarchy of the four values. In the analysis the method of paired comparisons described by Thurstone and others[4] was applied. A detailed description of the research procedure follows.

1) Six pairs of values were formed, pairing successively

each value with each other value, i.e., education with income; education with power; education with cultural consumption; income with power; income with cultural consumption; and cultural consumption with power.

2) From each of these pairs of general values, three pairs of corresponding specific values were singled out.[5]

3) These specific values were three levels of education, three levels of managerial positions, and several different income levels.

Cultural consumption signified the same thing in all naratives. Elementary, secondary, and higher education were differentiated. The positions of master craftsman, division manager, and director of an industrial enterprise were chosen to represent degrees of power. The choice of income level was determined by the other value with which it conflicted. This decision was completely arbitrary. The mean earnings of master craftsman, division manager, and director, and also of persons with basic vocational, secondary, technical, and higher education, were determined on the basis of previous studies on the social differentiation of Łódź residents. These data were used in constructing the narratives in which one of the values was income.

4) For each pair of specific values, a situational context was constructed in which these two values were in conflict.

Certain known patterns of incompatibility of the social status attributes were utilized in the narratives. Here are a few examples of these narratives. The symbol I denotes income, M denotes managerial position, E stands for education, and CC for cultural consumption.

$$I_1 - M_1$$

Franciszek A. was a master craftsman and earned 2,300 złotys. If he were to work in another division as a worker, he would make 2,700 złotys, but he would have to give up his managerial position. What should he do?

$$E_{111} - I_{111}$$

Andrzej I. lived in Katowice, finished high school, but did not go to college. Although he was a capable student, he was not accepted because of stiff competition. He started working in a coal mine and was making a good salary. After one year his pay was raised to 3,300 złotys because he proved to be a competent and valued worker. He therefore could not decide whether to try once more for admission to college, for he knew that after studies in his field he would make much less money — at most 2,500 złotys. In your opinion, what should his decision be?

$$E_1-M_1$$

Eugeniusz D. finished basic trade school and worked as a master craftsman in a radio plant. A modern division was built there, and workers with secondary technical education were needed to work in it. Eugeniusz had the opportunity to finish technical high school within three years and to work in the new division. He would not be a master craftsman, but only one of many employees. His pay would be similar to what he earned before. Should he sign up for the vocational high school course?

$$I_{11}-CC$$

Kazimierz M. is a technician and makes 2,400 złotys. His wife works and they have one child. The plant managers often offer him overtime work with good pay. Making the extra money does not allow him to attend the theater or cinema or read books and periodicals, all of which he enjoys very much. At each offer of additional work he experiences conflict because he knows that he will have to give up a book, play, or film. If he refused, however, he would no longer get such offers. Should he take additional work or not?

Hierarchy of the Four General Values

Each narrative contained two conflicting values. For each socio-occupational category the difference between the total number of choices of one value and the total number of choices of the other value was calculated for each of the sixteen pairs.

These data in turn were used to compute the mean differences of the total preference for each pair of conflicting general values in the whole sample.[6]

Table 1 shows these mean differences. We see that education was more highly preferred three times, and cultural consumption once. Managerial position did not receive higher preference even once. Therefore the four values are arranged in this order: (1) education; (2) income; (3) cultural consumption; and (4) managerial positions.

Table 1

Mean Differences in Preference of General Values
in the Whole Community

Pairs of conflicting general values	Value with higher number of preferences	Mean difference of preferences
Education–Cultural consumption	education	507.5
Education–Managerial positions	education	419.0
Education–Income	education	388.0
Income–Managerial positions	income	159.3
Income–Cultural consumption	income	158.3
Cultural consumption–Managerial positions	cultural consumption	101.5

Table 2, which shows the average differences in preferences for individual socio-occupational categories, indicates that the same values are more often preferred by all three groups: engineers, blue-collar workers, and artisans. In other words, all categories of respondents have the same hierarchy of the four general values.[7]

The narratives were constructed so as to rid each of the four values of their instrumental function, at least in relation to the three remaining values. For the most part we were concerned with the instrumentality of education in relation to income, and of managerial position relative to income. Thus a higher preference for education can be interpreted to mean that education is highly valued even if it does not result in higher incomes and higher positions.

162

Table 2

Mean Differences in Preference of General Values in Three Socio-occupational Categories

Pairs of conflicting general values	Engineers		Workers		Artisans	
	value with higher number of preferences	mean difference in preferences	value with higher number of preferences	mean difference in preferences	value with higher number of preferences	mean difference in preferences
Education–Cultural consumption	education	169.0	education	167.5	education	171.0
Education–Managerial positions	education	134.7	education	141.3	education	143.0
Education–Income	education	146.3	education	111.7	education	130.0
Income–Cultural consumption	income	90.7	income	30.3	income	37.3
Income–Managerial positions	income	71.7	income	51.7	income	36.0
Cultural consumption–Managerial positions	cultural consumption	36.5	cultural consumption	43.0	cultural consumption	22.0

It appears that we have resolved the difficult and recurrent problem of whether money or education is valued more highly by people. In view of the interdependence between education and income, it is usually difficult to answer this question. I will avoid the issue of motivation for seeking an education. A justifiable interpretation of the data would be that increasing the level of education without increasing pay is more valued than increasing income, but without an accompanying rise in education. This statement maintains its validity only up to certain limits, and we cannot overgeneralize it. At certain levels of both education and income the relative proportions of choices would probably change.

In turn we should consider what might cause the relatively low ranking of managerial positions in the value system. In the six pairs of conflicting general values, the managerial position did not predominate even once. It was preferred even less than so minimally instrumental a value as cultural consumption.

Intrinsic Value of Managerial Positions in Three Socioeconomic Categories

I will discuss the intrinsic value of managerial positions in the more restricted sense, that is, as the satisfaction stemming from the exertion of influence on the actions of others and the possibility of making important decisions. The following question was asked of the respondents: "Why do you think people seek managerial positions?" There was a choice of answers to this question which the interviewers did not read to the respondents. This served solely to classify the responses; but if an answer did not fit into any of the categories, it was recorded in full.

Among the values which people expect to achieve through managerial positions (Table 3), the engineers placed satisfaction and pleasure derived from power first, whereas artisans and workers ranked it second. People differ with respect to the need to dominate, the tendency to assume leadership, and

Table 3

Instrumental and Intrinsic Values of Managerial Positions by Socio-occupational Category (in %)

Socio-occupational category	Income	Special privileges	Public interest	Prestige	Personal satisfaction (intrinsic value of positions)	Other	Size of category (N)
Engineers	62.0	15.5	30.5	31.5	70.0	8.0	200
Workers	66.5	19.0	21.5	27.5	54.0	8.5	200
Artisans	61.0	20.5	23.5	27.5	54.5	6.5	200

T = .05; T' = .06.

165

the drive to subordinate other persons to themselves. These needs, tendencies, and drives, regardless of how they have been shaped, are characteristic only of certain individuals. The institutional hierarchy of authority creates opportunities to satisfy these power needs, since people who experience such needs have the opportunity to assume managerial positions. The exercise of authority constitutes a value in itself for them apart from other advantages related to it. Table 3 indicates that for 70.0% of the engineers, 54.0% of the workers, and 54.5% of the artisans, managerial positions have an intrinsic value. Summarizing, we can say that managerial positions operate primarily as an intrinsic value in people's consciousness. The causes for their lower prestige must lie elsewhere, and probably have something to do with their perceived instrumentality.

Instrumentality of Managerial Positions

The satisfaction that stems from exercising authority can be considered the index of its intrinsic value. Setting the intrinsic value aside, the instrumentality of authority is understood similarly in all three socio-occupational categories. Managerial positions are mainly expected to yield material advantages. Sixty-two percent of the engineers, 66.5% of the workers, and 61.0% of the artisans stated that managerial positions are valued because they increase the possibility of obtaining higher income (Table 3).

Once again, then, we encounter confirmation of the value of income. Income in turn is instrumental chiefly in relation to consumption values. Income is only an intrinsic value to a small extent, yet it remains a powerful motivating factor in human actions. Both education and managerial positions are perceived by the respondents primarily as means to higher income. The expectation is that by obtaining education and a managerial position, one will consequently receive a high salary. This conclusion applies equally to all socio-occupational categories.

Prestige, as a value which accompanies authority, was ranked second by all three categories of respondents (Table 3).

The value generally termed public interest was ranked a close third behind prestige. Performing managerial functions is considered a social service; undertaking tasks that are difficult and require responsibility tends to improve our lives.

Public interest, interpreted as socially oriented attitudes, is nonetheless superseded by the three values discussed above:

1) the fulfillment of ambitions and the satisfaction stemming from management;

2) higher income;

3) personal prestige.

These values can be considered elements of an egoistic attitude. The individual, not the society, constitutes their frame of reference.

It is worth noting, however, that engineers differ somewhat from the remaining two categories, not only because they interpret power more as an intrinsic value but also because they subordinate it to the public interest to a greater degree. Moreover, engineers expect fewer personal advantages apart from income and prestige. For example, foreign travel, easier access to rare and sought after goods and services on the market, advantageous connections, easier access to higher education for their children, better places of work, etc., were all advantages mentioned by the respondents.

Generally it can be said that the range of instrumentality of managerial positions in relation to positive values is not very large. The mean number of values which people expect to gain by means of power is 2.17 for engineers, 1.97 for blue-collar workers, and 1.93 for artisans. Power has a smaller "field of instrumentality" than, for example, education.

Income is included in this "field" and also plays the most important role in it. In forming the hierarchy of four general values in relation to income, power was deprived of instrumentality. Because income is higher in the hierarchy of values than managerial positions, we suspect that the number of choices of managerial positions would have increased if higher income had derived from it. Would managerial positions then assume

167

a place in the hierarchy higher than cultural consumption?
This question, unfortunately, cannot be answered. We can only
state that not allowing managerial position to influence an individual's income could lower the number of preferences for it.

Choice of the Most Attractive Managerial Position

The respondents were presented with the choice of four managerial positions: master craftsman, production division manager, director of an enterprise, and the general director of
several enterprises within a given industry, which we shall call
the executive director. The master craftsman is directly responsible to the production manager, the latter in turn to the
director of the enterprise, etc.

These positions, then, represent different levels of power,
and their attainment is related to various levels of competence
in handling a range of sanctions and responsibilities. The nature of activities involved in the range of responsibilities and
the type of qualifications and privileges are also different. Thus
moving up the hierarchy does not only imply increasing the
range of influence, importance of decisions, and amount of responsibility. It is also a "qualitative" change in the type of authority, going from leadership power in small formal groups to
bureaucratic authority that relies on indirect management and
influence through a multilevel and extensive administrative
structure. At a higher level of authority the direct relation of
the manager to the production process is decreased, and an increase in the coordination of tasks among specific units that
are indispensable to the proper functioning of the whole process
occurs. We can also note the increasing formalization of the
function, that is, the elimination of the effect of informal relations in the production process. Informality exists in the lower
levels because of the manager's direct cooperation with subordinate workers, and to some extent it determines the effectiveness of the managerial tasks performed.

The results of these studies show that each socio-occupa-

Table 4

The Most Attractive Managerial Position by Socio-occupational Category (in %)

Socio-occupational category	Master craftsman	Manager of production division	Director of enterprise	Executive director	Cannot decide	Chooses none	Size of category (100%)
Engineers	7.5	40.5	21.5	21.5	6.0	3.0	200
Workers	15.5	29.0	16.0	37.5	0.5	1.5	200
Artisans	31.0	28.0	13.5	22.5	4.0	1.0	200

T = 0.19; T' = 0.24.

169

tional category considers a different level of authority the most worthwhile (Table 4). Engineers prefer the position of production division manager, workers the position of executive director, and artisans the position of master craftsman. This is the first study in which such a considerable differentiation of choices has appeared. None of the positions received a decided majority of preferences, and the choices among positions are more uniformly distributed than the distribution of choices pertaining to the forms of cultural participation, the level of indispensable education, the income necessary for an affluent life, or the elements of material well-being.

Does a different type of rationale in each socio-occupational category go hand in hand with a differing preference for managerial positions? Let us look more closely at what attracts engineers to the position of production manager, workers to the position of executive director, and artisans to the position of master craftsman. The respondents were asked to justify their choice in the form of an answer to an open question.

Above all, artisans value three attributes characterizing a master craftsman's work. First of all, the master craftsman is most closely associated with the production process. He does not view production "from behind a desk" but personally supervises and controls its progress. Second, a master craftsman is a very good specialist with high qualifications. The artisans do not value managerial qualifications as much as those skills necessary to perform the work. In their opinion these skills should determine advancement to a managerial position; and at the same time, possession of them constitutes insurance in case of dismissal from this position. The third, most valuable characteristic attached to the position of master craftsman, according to the artisans, is immediate contact and cooperation with the work crew.

Thus the master craftsman is not just a managing figure who makes decisions affecting persons subordinate to him (a characteristic that is less important to the artisans). The artisans are not concerned with the possibility of manipulating people and being empowered to decide their fate, but rather with re-

170

maining within the collective, maintaining good relations in the
work group, and also with giving help and counsel to subordinate
workers in personal matters. For the master craftsman plays
an important role in both formal and informal relations. He is
more a leader, someone who also has personal authority, rather
than a "man of power" equipped with broad sanctions and far
reaching influence.

One can find specific characteristics of artisans' work in this
image of the master. They fill the role of heads of small teams
of workers. Only 15% of the sample of artisans work without
assistance. To this day the title of master signifies a professional title in craftsmanship. Models of the master craftsman
who works together with his students and apprentices, is the
best specialist, and also performs leadership functions, while
at the same time remaining their patron, have persisted in tradition. We can find a model of the master craftsman similar
to this one in the artisans' statements substantiating their
choice of it as the position most attractive to them.

The position of production manager, considered especially
worthwhile by the engineers, is also valuable because it is concerned with production work and necessitates having extensive
occupational knowledge. Thus it is valued for the same reasons
that artisans value the master's work. It is more important for
engineers, however, that the position of production manager enables them to demonstrate initiative and to apply professional
expertise in a creative way. The manager of production also
has a chance to exhibit his organizational abilities. This job
includes elements such as professionalism and more indepen-
dence, decision-making, and influence on production. At the
same time, this is work in production, not manipulation by directives and regulations.

The model of a manager that is particularly attractive to engineers is the manager-professional or the manager-expert,
who is oriented more to the accomplishment of concrete tasks
and less to performing the role of leader of the work crew.
This is also not a manager-administrator type.

For the workers who chose the position of executive director, income was the most attractive factor, as well as such other material privileges as official visits abroad or having a car for their own use. Another characteristic that makes this position very attractive to the workers is the broad range of the executive director's authority. Both the fates of the people and of whole branches of the economy depend on his decisions. At the same time, the workers think that exercising authority at this level is a much more pleasant function than work directly concerned with production. Far from the constant problems concerned with implementing the work plan, they feel that issuing directives and participating in meetings and conferences is not too difficult but is, rather, quite easy and pleasant. In their opinion difficult and heavy work, genuine effort, and overcoming adversities occur in lower positions. The satisfaction of ruling, status on the outside, the prestige associated with it, and appreciable material advantages accrue to the executive director.

As we see, the most attractive kind of managerial position is perceived by respondents in different ways. The attitudes of people who chose the same managerial positions are also differentiated by socio-occupational category. Different values related to the same position are ranked first by each of the socio-occupational categories.

Instrumentality of Managerial Positions in Relation to Negative Values

Respondents also associated managerial positions with an appreciable number of negative values. Characteristically some of these negative values constitute positive values for other persons. In general, industriousness, responsibility in carrying out difficult tasks, and work performed individually are recognized and appreciated values. For certain people these are negative values, whereas positive values include: little responsibility, "doing nothing," small amount of work, absence of duties, taking on easy tasks not connected with overcoming difficulties, diverting work to others, and receiving high wages for it. In certain instances these values determined the choice of a given level of authority.

We are not concerned here with the correctness of the respondents' characterization of specific positions but with the fact that merit is attributed to these antivalues when people praise indolence, lack of responsibility, lack of conscientiousness in work, and so on.

Certain negative values with respect to managerial positions never appear as positive values. They are work that is too stressful, especially in higher positions, and a lack of job security, with resulting anxiety. Another negative value is performing nonproduction managerial functions, where specialized qualifications are not required and which can be performed by persons with a general education. Advancement in this case does not depend on specialized knowledge. People who have occupational training in a given area of production are employed in the positions of master craftsman and division head. Individuals of whom no strictly defined training is required are often employed in the position of manager of an administrative division, firm, or group of enterprises. And even if they do possess specific qualifications, after some period of time spent in administrative work, their occupational skills decrease appreciably. When one stops performing a managerial function, one does not even retain a trace of definite managerial qualifications. The time is often considered lost in terms of a further occupational career. The respondents value occupational stability highly because they believe that every successive phase of work should include an increase in training, an improvement in occupational position, or heightened labor market chances, etc. At the same time, assuming managerial positions, especially outside production, gives some kind of satisfaction, higher pay, prestige, or other privileges, which, however, are not permanent. Losing one's position not only hurts personal ambition but generates the feeling that the previously exerted effort was a poor "investment" that will not further one's career.

Jadwiga Koralewicz-Zębik

Conclusion

My studies have shown that similarities outweigh differences among the value systems of different socio-occupational categories. This is evidence of the cultural integration that is occurring in our society. Since the three socio-occupational categories represent different segments of the class-stratum structure, I relate the similarities among them to the cultural integration taking place among the basic classes in a large city. These aspects of a common value system were identified:

a) A unification of the value hierarchy has taken place among socio-occupational categories. The hierarchial order of the general values in this study is: (1) education; (2) income; (3) cultural consumption; and (4) managerial positions. Hierarchies of specific values also exhibit great similarity.

b) The instrumentality of specific values is similarly perceived by each of the socio-occupational categories. This does not mean that there are no differences among the categories, nor does it mean that those which appear are of secondary importance.

Least consensus was found on the value of managerial positions. Observing the socio-occupational categories in relation to this value, we found that managerial positions were ranked last in the hierarchy, and that this was associated with an appreciable divergence of choices in a value-conflict situation. Managerial positions were negatively assessed more often than education, income, or cultural consumption.

Notes

1. In general there are few empirical studies of value systems in Poland. Those that have been done were conducted among secondary school and university youths and also in rural areas, small towns, and a few factories. Compare Z. Sufin and W. Wesołowski, "Miejsce pracy w hierarchii wartości," Kultura i społeczeństwo 4 (1963); I. Nowak, "Samoocena i vsposobienie a wartości (studium porównawcze dwóch środowisk studenckich)," Studia socjologiczne 2 (1966); A. P. Wejland, "Autorytet rodziców i rodzinna wspólnota wartości," Studia Socjolo-

giczne 3 (1970); A. Kłoskowska, "Wartości, potrzeby i aspiracje kulturalne małej społeczności miejskiej," Studia Socjologiczne 3 (1970); Z. Sufin, "Le travail en tant que valeur sociale," Transformations de la campagne polonaise, R. Turski, ed. (Wrocław, 1970); D. Dobrowolska, "Praca zawodowa jako wartość dla przedstawicieli różnych klas i kategorii zawodowych," Studia Socjologiczne 3 (1972).

2. I base this statement on unpublished results of studies by A. Sarapata. These studies were conducted in 1966 on a representative sample of the inhabitants of Szczecin. I cite them with the author's permission.

3. Cultural consumption as a characteristic of social standing is different in nature from education, income, and position. It is a secondary characteristic of social status. It also seems to have a somewhat different character as a value. Income, education, and position are ends as well as means to each other, but cultural consumption has only intrinsic value. It almost never is a means.

4. See L. L. Thurstone, The Measurement of Values (Chicago 1959), chapter entitled "The Method of Paired Comparisons for Social Values." This method was also described by J. P. Guilford, Psychometric Methods (New York, 1954), in his chapter "The Method of Paired Comparisons."

5. The lowest level of cultural consumption was not compared with the lowest level of power and the lowest level of education. In pilot studies it was found that respondents unanimously chose managerial positions and education over cultural consumption on this lowest level. Cultural consumption does not constitute a conflict value, and the narratives were interpreted as rather absurd. For this reason they were not used in the main studies. In all there were sixteen narratives, and there would have been eighteen if each of the six pairs of general values had been represented by three narratives.

6. The mean difference in preferences was calculated in the following way: the difference of preferences was summed on all levels within each pair of general values for the whole population, and then this sum was divided by the number of levels. Because two levels were differentiated in the conflict of education with cultural consumption and managerial positions with cultural consumption, the sum obtained was divided by two, whereas the remaining sums were divided by three. The numbers obtained in this way can be compared to each other. The maximum mean value of difference in preferences is 600.

7. These mean differences in preference have been calculated in the same way as for the whole population. The modification consists solely in that the difference in preferences was summed not for the whole population but for each socio-occupational category. Because of this the maximum difference of preferences is 200.

Krzysztof Ostrowski

LABOR UNIONS AND THE WORKING CLASS:
AN ANALYSIS OF PARTICIPATION IN POWER*

In Poland, as in all socialist countries, there is only one labor union in each firm rather than several based on occupational affiliations. The employees in a given work place are
members of a local union organization that belongs to one of 23
national labor unions. This eliminates the partitioning of the
union movement into numerous unions that would otherwise exist in one firm. The work place, and not the occupational group,
becomes the basis for integrating members of a union. The
place of work is also the basis for forming party and other sociopolitical organizations. Thus the work place in the socialist
system not only performs economic functions but is also the
forum for political action.

The basic organizational unit for all unions is the firm's
union organization. It can be made up of as few as 20 employees or of more than 10,000. In larger firms there are sectional
union organizations subordinate to the firm's union organization. Sectional union organizations involve specific departments,
divisions, or other organizational units of the firm. Union
groups subordinate to the sectional organizations and including
between 10 and several dozen employees are organized on the
basis of commonly performed work.

*From Krzysztof Ostrowski, Rola związków zawodowych w polskim
systemie politycznym (Wrocław: Ossolineum, 1970), pp. 49, 61, 68-84,
and 87-89. Abridgements and minor editorial changes were introduced
by the editors with the author's consent.

Labor Unions and the Working Class

The Representation Process in Labor Unions

Similar to the party and other sociopolitical organizations, labor unions elect their governing bodies by indirect or direct voting. By creating opportunities for political activity, the representation system involves great numbers of people in the governing process. The representation system has created a very broad base of political activity in People's Poland. The activities of people's councils involve more than 170,000 persons in the council groups and nearly 250,000 persons in commissions. Almost 300,000 elective offices exist in the party structure, and worker self-government is operated by more than 230,000 activists (i.e., those individuals who hold voluntary, usually elective, positions). The union movement, however, involves the largest activist group. Labor unions have over one million elective offices, and more than 8 million employees are members of 23 unions.

An elected activist bloc creates a barrier to the stabilization and professionalization of the management of each political institution. The increasing complexity of political work, the increasing range of problems, and the constant improvement of methods of operation could produce a greater specialization of the activists primarily through stabilization of the activist bloc and the development of salaried positions. However, a tendency toward rapid turnover in the activist bloc, and also a tendency to replace salaried positions by volunteer work whenever possible, are quite evident in the socialist political system.

In the 1966 elections 57.3% new chairmen of firm councils, 54.8% new members of firm councils, 67.2% new members of section councils, and 67.2% new members of the activist bloc were elected to leadership positions in union organizations. Thus despite the large number of positions in firms' union organizations, more than 50% of the activist bloc is replaced after a two-year term.

The number of salaried positions in political organizations was considerably reduced at the end of the 1950s. In labor unions the salaried political workers numbered over 10,000 persons in 1950, over 5,000 in 1955, and 2,183 in 1963. With

more than 32,000 enterprise union organizations and nearly
1,500 union officials, a group of several thousand salaried
workers is the indispensable minimum necessary to insure ef-
ficient functioning of the complex union structure.[1]

In large enterprises labor unions also wield the power to give
members of the firm councils leave from their occupational
duties, thereby permitting complete involvement in union work.
A few years ago almost 10,000 members of firm councils were
involved in this form of leave; but lately there has been a tight-
ening of regulations concerning leave privileges, and it has been
increasingly stressed that union activity should consist mostly
of voluntary work combined with the daily work routine.

The elected union activist bloc is very large, and its base is
primarily the firm. The avoidance of stabilization and professionalization of the activist bloc indicates that the representation system is intended primarily to serve the interests of the
large masses of union members. However, the question should
be asked: How is the representation of the membership achieved
through the elections of leaders at various levels?

We have chosen the analysis of worker participation in the
activist bloc of firms' union organizations to assess the equitability of representation in labor unions. The firm union organization has undergone a gradual but decided reduction in activist bloc membership, ranging from several hundred thousand
in the union groups to thirty thousand heads of firm union councils. The increasing complexity of union functions within the
plants leads us to believe that the percentage of workers who
hold positions in unions will be differentiated both among unions
and among positions. The problem considered in this analysis
is to establish whether the degree of worker participation in
union leadership is predictable, that is, if it can be discovered
through an analysis of the extent of worker participation at various levels and in various unions.

The amount of worker participation in the activist bloc is
shown in Table 1.

Both on a nationwide scale and on the average in specific
unions, there is less worker participation at higher levels in

178

Labor Unions and the Working Class

Table 1

Participation of Workers in the Leadership
of the Firm Union Organization

	Total	Workers	% workers	% workers in union (on average)
	in thousands		workers	
Employees	7,922.2	4,947.5	62.5	60.4
Labor union members	7,662.7	4,730.1	61.7	58.9
Activist bloc of union groups	388.7	251.1	64.6	60.6
Stewards	155.3	92.9	59.8	59.8
Members of section councils	83.9	58.5	69.7	54.3
Heads of section councils	15.3	10.4	68.0	51.9
Members of firm councils	240.0	82.7	34.5	40.1
Heads of firm councils	32.2	9.3	28.8	31.6

the union organization. Whereas union groups or sectional organizations directly involve various worker groups, the firm councils (which generally direct all problems and activities of the firm) are based on uniform, not proportional, participation of various worker groups. On the average 27% of firm council chairmen in production unions are administrative workers, and 31% are engineering-technical workers.

Is there a correlation between the proportions of workers at successive levels in the hierarchy of the firm across unions? The correlation matrix in Table 2 indicates that there is indeed a strong relationship.

Knowing that the concentration of workers at a given level of the structure in a given union is higher than in another union, we can say with a very high degree of probability that the difference between these unions will be maintained at all other levels. Moreover, knowing the percentage of workers among the total employed will enable us to derive with a high degree of probability the proportion of workers in union leadership relative to other unions. Let us note, however, that the correlation of the proportion of workers is particularly high between neighboring levels in the structure, whereas this correlation gradually decreases with the increasing distance between levels

179

Krzysztof Ostrowski

Table 2

Correlations of Proportions of Workers Participating
in the Leadership of Firm Union Organizations
(Pearson's correlation coefficients)

Forms of participation*	Forms of participation						
	1	2	3	4	5	6	7
1		0.99	0.98	0.97	0.95	0.96	0.88
2			0.99	0.94	0.93	0.94	0.85
3				0.94	0.92	0.92	0.83
4					0.99	0.97	0.89
5						0.98	0.92
6							0.96
7							

*1. worker employees; 2. worker group activist bloc; 3 worker
stewards; 4. worker members of sectional councils; 5. worker heads
of sectional councils; 6. worker members of firm councils; 7. worker
heads of firm councils.

Table 3

Range of Worker Participation in the Leadership
of Firm Union Organization

Worker participation	(a) Mean percentage of workers	(b) Standard deviation	$\frac{b}{a} \times 100$
Total employed	60.4	23.6	39.1
Activist bloc of union groups	60.6	30.0	49.7
Stewards	59.8	28.7	48.8
Section council members	54.3	28.6	52.8
Heads of section councils	51.9	29.9	57.6
Members of firm councils	40.1	22.0	54.7
Heads of firm councils	31.6	21.2	67.2

compared. Thus, for example, the correlations of proportion
of workers among total employees with proportion of workers
at successive levels of the union hierarchy are 0.99, 0.98, 0.97,
0.96, and 0.88 (see the top row of Table 2).

180

Labor Unions and the Working Class

The above differences, although slight, require further analysis, since it happens that the probability of correctly explaining worker concentration decreases when progressively more differentiated levels of the structure are compared. Let us first compare the differences between unions at successive levels of the structure. They are given in Table 3.

Comparison of the mean percentage with the standard deviation shows that the higher the level of union structure, the larger the differentiation among the unions.

Figure 1 shows worker participation in the leadership of several unions. It appears that the tendency toward reduced worker participation has various manifestations in different unions. Thus, for example, appreciable differences in filling the position of firm council chairman are found in unions with similar percentages of workers among total employees: amalgamated local industries, mining, printing, agriculture, and textile.

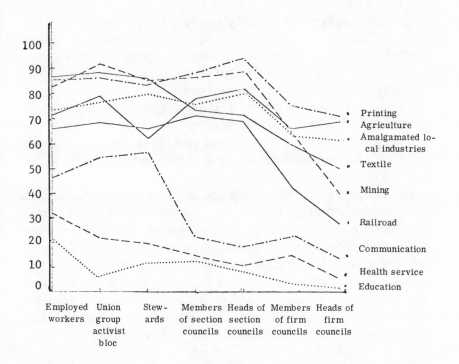

The differentiation of specific unions emphasized above explains the nature of the representation process in various environments. Can the uniformity of worker participation at successive levels of the structure be used to predict the pattern of representation in various labor unions? If so, then the prediction of worker concentration in the union leadership would be evidence of the equitability of the representation process in the union movement as a whole.

Multiple regression analysis makes it possible to predict the concentration of a given characteristic from the distribution of several other characteristics. We will use regression analysis in order to examine the outcomes of the representation process in particular unions. Let us assume that the participation of workers at all levels of the firm union hierarchy is known. How accurately can we assess the percentage of worker participation among the total employed on the basis of this information? The regression equation is:

$$\bar{y} = b_1 x_1 + b_2 x_2 + b_3 x_3 + b_4 x_4 + b_5 x_5 + b_6 x_6,$$

where $\bar{y}$ = estimated percentage of workers among the employees;

x_1 = % workers in the activist bloc of union groups;
x_2 = % workers among stewards;
x_3 = % workers among section council members;
x_4 = % workers among section council heads;
x_5 = % workers among firm council members;
x_6 = % workers among firm council heads;
$b_1 \ldots b_6$ — regression coefficients.

The comparison of estimated and observed values for specific labor unions, ordered in a sequence of decreasing worker participation among total employees, is presented in Table 4. The regression of worker participation at different levels of the union structure allows us to estimate the percentage of workers among the total employees with a generally high degree of accuracy. This verifies the equitability of the worker representation process in union leadership. The estimated values are particularly accurate for unions with considerable proportions

Table 4

Participation of Workers among Total Employees
Predicted by Regression

Unions	% workers among total employees		Difference $y - \bar{y}$	Ratio $\dfrac{\bar{y}}{y} \times 100$
	observed value y	estimated value $\bar{y}$		
Textile	86.6	87.1	−0.5	100.6
Printing	85.0	86.4	−1.4	101.7
Mining	83.4	87.4	−4.0	104.8
Chemical	79.6	74.1	5.4	93.2
Foundry	78.3	79.3	−1.0	101.3
Forestry	75.2	76.1	−0.9	101.3
Construction	74.1	74.2	−0.1	100.2
Transport	73.5	75.8	−2.3	103.1
Metal	73.0	73.8	−0.8	101.2
Amalgamated local industries	72.6	71.6	1.0	98.6
Food processing	72.1	76.3	−4.2	105.8
Agriculture	72.0	67.9	4.1	94.3
Marine	70.5	69.7	0.8	98.9
Energy	66.1	69.7	−3.6	105.5
Railroad	65.7	63.3	2.4	96.3
Communication	46.3	48.4	−2.1	104.6
Commerce	37.7	37.8	−0.1	100.2
Culture and art	33.4	24.2	9.2	72.4
Health service	32.9	23.1	9.8	70.2
Education	22.9	7.2	15.1	32.4
Mass media	14.7	5.1	9.6	34.7
Government	14.4	10.3	4.1	71.7

of workers. The accuracy prediction, however, is much less
in a few nonproduction unions, where the percentage of workers
estimated on the basis of the representation process is lower
than that actually observed.

Another question is: How accurately can one predict the participation of workers in union groups and section and firm councils knowing only the percentage of workers among total em-

183

Table 5

Ratios of Estimated to Observed Values of Worker Participation
in the Leadership of Firm Union Organizations (in %)

Unions and members (in thousands)		Group activist bloc	Stewards	Members of section councils	Heads of section councils	Members of firm councils	Heads of firm councils
Textile	584.4	101	100	109	111	101	101
Printing	46.2	101	102	90	83	78	66
Mining	613.1	96	96	89	87	96	124
Chemical	383.0	105	103	112	111	105	94
Foundry	287.2	95	96	99	95	98	113
Forestry	214.7	94	92	93	98	113	114
Construction	705.7	97	92	95	94	102	96
Transport	229.3	100	97	100	102	100	105
Metal	785.8	100	104	104	102	97	106
Amalgamated local industries	551.2	100	94	90	82	85	69
Food processing	853.8	103	102	96	100	93	96
Agriculture	544.6	95	115	87	81	87	60
Marine	111.7	98	99	99	104	116	142
Energy	127.7	90	94	114	137	114	102
Railroad	449.1	100	104	87	87	107	126
Communications	157.7	89	84	190	243	154	253
Commerce	902.8	141	126	93	123	132	219
Culture and art	71.4	111	111	221	241	236	466
Health service	412.6	165	168	221	280	170	316
Education	496.8	385	237	198	226	774	6,220
Government	304.3	317	334	138	210	130	141

Labor Unions and the Working Class

ployees? Table 5 shows the ratios of estimated to observed
values, multiplied by 100, which represent the participation of
workers at specific levels based on the known percentage of
workers among the total employees. In certain production
unions (unions of textile workers, chemists, metal workers,
railroad employees) the percentage of workers among total employees enables us to predict accurately the percentages of
workers at increasingly higher levels of the union hierarchy.
In other unions (printers, agricultural workers, workers in
amalgamated local industries) worker participation is higher
than predicted, and in yet others (forestry workers, foundry
workers, miners), particularly in firm councils, worker participation is lower than expected. Thus whereas the situation in
production unions is indeed differentiated, the accuracy of pre-
dictions is relatively high. In nonproduction unions, however,
the representation at successive levels deviates from the general trend of all unions, that is, the trend is toward reduced
worker participation.

If worker participation can be treated as an index of the importance of the working class in the representation system,
then we can assume that a high proportion of workers in union

Table 6

Correlation of the Proportion of Workers and of PUWP
Members in the Leadership of Firm Union Organization*

Level	Pearson's correlation coefficient between the proportion of workers and the proportion of PUWP members
Activist bloc of union groups	0.376
Stewards	0.442
Members of section councils	0.595
Heads of section councils	0.507
Members of plant councils	0.421
Heads of plant councils	0.310

*The correlation coefficient is significant at the 0.05 level for
$r > 0.42$.

185

leadership should be correlated with a high proportion of union members in the Polish United Workers Party (PUWP). This correlation is shown in Table 6 for a selected sample of union structures within firms.

The direction of the relationship is the same for all levels of firm structure: the larger the number of workers, the larger the number of PUWP members. The joint occurrence of various characteristics in the representation process requires a more detailed study conducted on a broader data base. We shall try to determine whether the investigated characteristics of the representation process extend beyond the participation of workers in union leadership. A positive answer would indicate that some characteristics of the representation process can be generalized to the political system as a whole.

This thesis can be partially tested by comparing selected characteristics of union leadership and workers council leadership, that is, the proportion of workers and the proportion of PUWP members. We can ask the question: Is there a relationship between representation in union leadership and in the leadership of worker self-government? The object of the comparisons is the total representation in these structures and not correlations at particular levels.

Canonical correlation allows us to make this comparison and makes it possible to determine the correlation between two sets of variables. The level of significance can be determined by the F-test or the chi-square test. The results of canonical correlation for the proportion of PUWP members and workers in the leadership of worker self-government and in union leadership in 15 production unions are given in Table 7.

The comparison of the representation processes in two structures shows that the correlation is high and statistically significant. This indicates that the representation processes in socialist democracy reflect the characteristics of the electorate.

These analyses were primarily concerned with the problems of worker participation at various levels of the union structure. This is a vital problem in the analysis of the socialist system. The demonstrated interdependence of worker participation in

Labor Unions and the Working Class

Table 7

Correlation of Representation in the Leadership
of Worker Councils and Union Councils

Set I (criteria) Members of section councils, heads of section councils, members of firm councils, heads of firm councils			Set II (predictors) Members of section worker councils, heads of section worker councils, members of worker councils, heads of worker councils		
Representation in leadership	canonical correlation coefficient	chi square	degrees of freedom	probability
Workers	0.923	29.57	16	0.035
PUWP Members	0.942	34.39	16	0.009

different organizations shows that firms with high proportions
of workers have higher probabilities of delegating large groups
of their representatives to active sociopolitical work. This
finding is evidence of the importance of the working class in
our democracy despite contentions about the inevitability of
bureaucratization or increasing elitism of the contemporary
political process.

Note

1. Problems of the social activist bloc and the professional employees in political organizations in the socialist system were presented
in more depth elsewhere. For example, see the article by J. Wiatr and
K. Ostrowski, "Political Leadership: What Kind of Professionalism,"
in J. Wiatr, ed., Studies in the Polish Political System (Wrocław, 1967).

BIBLIOGRAPHY

Adamski, Władysław

1965. "Dwa modele struktury i stosunków społecznych wsi" [Two models of the structure and social relations in villages]. Studia Socjologiczne 4: 169-96.

1971. Determinanty aktywności społecznej [Determinants of social activities]. Warsaw: Państwowe Wydawnictwo Naukowe.

Aleksa, Ludwik

1969. Pochodzenie społeczne i rekrutacja środowiskowa wybranej grupy inżynierów [Social origins and recruitment of a selected group of engineers]. Katowice: Śląski Instytut Naukowy.

Babinski, Grzegorz

1975. "Społeczno-demograficzne determinanty poglądów i postaw studentów" [Sociodemographic determinants of beliefs and attitudes of college students]. Życie Szkoły Wyższej 9: 51-61.

Balicki, Andrzej

Stabilność kadr pracowniczych [The stability of personnel]. Warsaw: Państwowe Wydawnictwo Ekonomiczne.

Bazylewski, Wiktor, and Krystyna Ciechocinska

1966. Analiza spożycia usług w różnych środowiskach społecznych na podstawie budżetów rodzinnych [Analysis of the use of services in several social groups based on family budgets]. Warsaw: Instytut Przemysłu Drobnego i Rzemiosła.

Beskid, Lidia

1963. "Poziom realny dochodów ludności pracowniczej w Polsce w roku 1960 w porównaniu z rokiem 1937" [The real level of incomes of the working population in Poland in 1960 in comparison with 1937]. Przegląd Statystyczny 3.

1976. "Stopien rozpiętości płac realnych netto w Polsce w okresie 1952-1972" [The range of real net wages in Poland during 1952-1972]. In Lidia Beskid and Zbigniew Sufin, eds., Ekonomiczne i społeczne problemy spożycia. Wrocław: Ossolineum.

Beskid, Lidia, and Krzysztof Zagórski

1971. Robotnicy na tle przemian struktury społecznej w Polsce [Workers and the transformation of social structure in Poland. Warsaw: Głowny Urząd Statystyczny.

Bibliography

Białecki, Ireneusz

1975. "Społeczne mechanizmy rekrutacji do zawodów wymagających wyższego wykształcenia" [Social mechanisms of recruitment to occupations requiring higher education]. Dydaktyka Szkoły Wyższej 4(32): 17-28.

1976. "Wykształcenie a wybór zawodu" [Education and occupational choice]. Kultura i Społeczenstwo 4: 191-204.

Bielecki, Franciszek

1968. Poziom wykształcenia i wysokość płac w gospodarce uspołecznionej w Polsce [Levels of education and income in the socialized economy of Poland]. Wrocław: Ossolineum.

Bielicki, Wacław

1967. "Niektóre elementy kultury robotniczej w świetle badan w trzech wybranych środowiskach przemysłowych" [Some aspects of workers' culture, based on research in three industries]. Socjologiczne Problemy Przemysłu i Klasy Robotniczej 2: 86-99.

Błuszkowski, Jan, and Włodzimierz Wesołowski

1976. "Przemiany struktury społecznej w Polsce Ludowej" [Transformations of social structure in Poland]. Pokolenia 1: 45-74.

Bokszanski, Zbigniew

1973. "Problematyka ruchliwości kulturowej" [Problems of cultural mobility]. Kultura i Społeczenstwo 17: 123-38.

1973. "O problematyce barier w procesie awansu kulturalnego robotników" [On the problem of barriers in the cultural advancement of workers]. Studia Etnograficzne 41-51.

1974. "Uwagi o koncepcji awansu kulturalnego" [Some remarks on the concept of cultural advancement]. Studia Socjologiczne 2: 187-96.

Bokszanski, Zbigniew, Jolanta Kulpinska, and Jan Woskowski

1975. Współczesna polska klasa robotnicza [Contemporary Polish working class]. Warsaw: Książka i Wiedza.

Bonkowicz-Sittauer, Jerzy

1966. "Dalsza nauka młodzieży wiejskiej po szkole podstawowej" [Education of rural youth after graduation from primary school]. Wieś Współczesna 10: 122-28.

Borowicz, Ryszard

1974. "Młodzież wiejska na studiach" [Rural youth in the schools of higher education]. Wieś Współczesna 18: 119-24.

1976. "Dostęp do szkoły wyższej w Polsce" [Access to schools of higher education in Poland]. Wieś i Rolnictwo 4(13): 56-66.

Borowski, Stanisław

1968. "Wielkość rodziny chłopskiej w Polsce Ludowej" [Size of farmer families in Poland]. Studia Demograficzne 15: 79-92.

Borucki, Andrzej

1967. Kariery zawodowe i postawy społeczne inteligencji w PRL, 1945-1959 [Occupational careers and attitudes of the intelligentsia in Poland, 1945-1959]. Wrocław: Ossolineum.

1975. "Struktura społeczna w świadomości mieszkanców miast. Problematyka i niektóre wyniki badan" [Social structure in the consciousness of city dwellers. Problems and research results]. Zeszyty Badan Rejonów Uprzemysłowionych 61: 193-207.

Bursche, Krystyna
1973. Awans robotników w zakładzie przemysłowym [Advancement of workers in an industrial plant]. Warsaw: Państwowe Wydawnictwo Ekonomiczne.

Chałasinski, Jósef
1958. Przeszłość i przyszłość inteligencji polskiej [Past and future of the Polish intelligentsia]. Warsaw: Państwowe Wydawnictwo Naukowe.

Chałasinski, Jósef (ed.)
1964. Awans pokolenia. Młode pokolenie wsi Polski Ludowej. Pamiętniki [The advance of a generation. The new generation in Polish villages. Memoirs]. Warsaw: Ludowa Spółdzielnia Wydawnicza.

1967. Od chłopa do rolnika. Młode pokolenie wsi Polski Ludowej. Pamiętniki [From peasant to farmer. The new generation in Polish villages. Memoirs]. Warsaw: Ludowa Spółdzielnia Wydawnicza.

1969. Nowe zawody. Młode pokolenie wsi Polski Ludowej. Pamiętniki [New occupations. The new generation in Polish villages. Memoirs]. Warsaw: Ludowa Spółdzielnia Wydawnicza.

1972. Drogi awansu w mieście. Młode pokolenie wsi Polski Ludowej. Pamiętniki [Paths to advancement in the cities. The new generation in Polish villages. Memoirs]. Warsaw: Ludowa Spółdzielnia Wydawnicza.

Chmielewska, Bożena
1970. Społeczno-kulturowe mechanizmy i kierunki awansu młodego pokolenia [Sociocultural mechanisms and the directions of advancement of the young generation]. Poznan: Wydawnictwo Poznanskie.

Chojka, Jan
1975. "Problemy społeczne ludności dwuzawodowej. Perspektywy młodzieży" [Social problems of bi-occupational population. Problems of youth]. Polityka Społeczna 10/22: 28-31.

Ciechocinska, Maria
1974. "Kierunki zmian w strukturze społecznej współczesnej Warszawy" [Changes in the social structure of contemporary Warsaw]. Studia Socjologiczne 1(52): 245-58.

Czauderska, Danuta
1975. "Czas wolny robotników" [Leisure time of workers]. Górnoslaskie Studia Socjologiczne 11: 187-229.

Czeczerda, Wanda
1964. Warunki i życzenia mieszkaniowe różnych grup ludności [Housing conditions of various population groups]. Warsaw: Arkady.

Czerniewska, Maria
1966. "Poziom życiowy rodzin chłopskich" [Standard of living of farmers' families]. Wieś Współczesna 10: 11-23.

Czyżowska, Zdzisława
1975. "Przemiany w pozycji społecznej kobiet w Polsce" [Changes in the social position of women in Poland]. Nowe Drogi 3(310): 40-50.

Dach, Zofia
1976. Praca zawodowa kobiet w Polsce w latach 1950-1972 i jej aspekty ekonomiczno-społeczne [Occupations of women in Poland, 1950-1972, and their socioeconomic aspects]. Warsaw: Książka i Wiedza.

Bibliography

1976. "Wykształcenie a aktywizacja zawodowa kobiet" [Education and occupational encouragement of women]. Gospodarka Planowa 11(367):
616-20.

Danecki, Jan
1958. Klasy, procesy klasowe i polityka klasowa we współczesnej Polsce
[Classes, class processes and class politics in contemporary Poland].
Warsaw: Książka i Wiedza.
1971. "Uwagi o stanie socjologii makrostruktur" [Remarks on the state of
macrostructural sociology]. Studia Socjologiczne 4.

Dąbrowska, Grażyna
1976. "Struktura zawodowa a struktura kształcenia ponadpodstawowego w
Płocku" [Occupational structure and postelementary education in
Płock]. Zeszyty Badania Rejonów Uprzemysławianych 63: 128-73.

Dobrowolska, Danuta
1963. Robotnicy na wczasach w pierwszych latach Polski Ludowej [Workers
on vacation during the first years of postwar Poland]. Wrocław:
Ossolineum.
1968. Przeobrażenia społeczne wsi podmiejskiej [Social changes in villages
near cities]. Wrocław: Ossolineum.
1972. "Praca zawodowa jako wartość dla różnych klas i kategorii zawodowych"[Work as value for various classes and occupational categories].
Studia Socjologiczne 3(46): 165-96.
1973. "Praca zawodowa jako wartość dla przedstawicieli różnych klas i kategorii zawodowych" [Work as a value for people from various classes
and occupational categories]. Studia Socjologiczne 3.

Drążkiewicz, Jerzy
1974. "Uwagi o aktywności społecznej i zróżnicowaniu społecznym" [Remarks
on voluntary activities and social differentiation]. Studia Socjologiczne
4(55): 173-90.

Drozdek, Zygmunt, and Eugenia Górniak
1969. "Losy absolwentów szkół wyższych, średnich i zasadniczych zawodowych, zatrudnionych w zakładach przemysłu ciężkiego i maszynowego"
[Careers of graduates of colleges, secondary schools, and trade
schools employed in the heavy and machine industries]. Studia i
Materiały Instytutu Pracy 61: 8-129.

Dyoniziak, Ryszard
1968. "Awans społeczny a poczucie sukcesu lub zawodu życiowego" [Social
advancement and the feeling of success or failure]. Ruch Prawniczy,
Ekonomiczny i Socjologiczny 30: 253-70.
1969. Zróżnicowanie kulturowe społeczności wielkomiejskiej [Cultural differentiation in a metropolitan community]. Warsaw: Państwowe
Wydawnictwo Ekonomiczne.

Dziewicka, Maria
1965. "W sprawie struktury społeczenstwa socjalistycznego" [On the structure of a socialist society]. Studia Socjologiczne 4: 5-14.
1975. "Dwuzawodowość w rolnictwie polskim" [Bi-occupational persons in
Polish agriculture]. Rocznik Socjologiczny Wsi, 1972-1974 12:
45-55.

Dzięcielska, Stefania
1962. Społeczna sytuacja dziennikarzy polskich [Social situation of Polish journalists]. Wrocław: Ossolineum.
Feldman, Wanda
1965. "Czynniki relacji płac mężczyzn i kobiet" [Factors influencing wage levels of men and women]. Zeszyty Naukowe Szkoły Głównej Planowania i Statystyki 57: 52-82.
Fotowicz, Bogumiła
1966. "Młodzież rejonu płockiego. Plany życiowe i ich realizacja w pierwszym roku po ukonczeniu szkoły podstawowej" [Płock region youth: life plans and their realization during the first year after graduation from primary school]. Biuletyn Instytutu Gospodarstwa Społecznego 9: 27-49.
Frąckowski, Roman
1976. "Zdrowie i ochrona zdrowia a zróżnicowanie społeczne" [Health, medical care, and social differentiation]. Studia Socjologiczne 3(62): 201-14.
Frieske, Kazimierz
1973. "Pozycja społeczna jako modyfikator postaw moralnych i prawnych" [Social position as a modifier of moral and legal attitudes]. Prace Instytutu Nauk Ekonomiczno-Społecznych Politechniki Warszawskiej 3: 107-28.
Fryzlewicz, Zofia
1975. "Przeobrażenia demograficznej i społeczno-zawodowej struktury ludności wsi" [Transformations of the demographic and socio-occupational structure of the rural population]. Wieś Współczesna 19: 72-82.
Galant, Wawrzyniec
1976. "Trzy pokolenia rodziny chłopskiej" [Three generations of rural families]. Wieś Współczesna 20: 106-12.
Gałdzicki, Zdzisław
1971. Przedsiębiorstwo jako układ stosunków społecznych i grup społeczno-zawodowych pracowników [The factory as a system of social relations and socio-occupational groups of employees]. Wrocław: Ossolineum.
Gałęski, Bogusław
1962. Społeczna struktura wsi. Problematyka i metoda badan [The social structure of the country. Research problems and methods]. Warsaw: Państwowe Wydawnictwo Naukowe.
1963. "Niektóre problemy struktury społecznej w świetle badan wiejskich" [Some problems of social structure in the light of rural research]. Studia Socjologiczne 1.
1963. "Zawód jako kategoria socjologiczna. Formowanie się zawodu rolnika" [Occupation as a sociological category. Emergence of the occupation of farmer]. Studia Socjologiczne 3.
1973. Studia nad społeczna struktura wsi [Studies in village social structure]. Wrocław: Ossolineum.
Gawronska, Władysława
1965. "Sytuacja mieszkaniowa ludności Płocka według grup społeczno-zawodowych" [Housing conditions of the Płock population by socio-

Bibliography

occupational groups]. Biuletyn Instytutu Gospodarstwa Społecznego 8: 73-83.

Głowacka, Maria, and Kazimierz Dziewo
1976. "Kadry kwalifikowane i ich wykorzystanie" [Highly qualified personnel and their employment]. Nowe Drogi 5(324): 126-36.

Goban-Klass, Tomasz
1971. Młodzi robotnicy Nowej Huty jako odbiorcy i współtwórcy kultury [Young workers of Nowa Huta as consumers and cocreators of culture]. Wrocław: Ossolineum.

Golachowski, Stefan
1969. "Struktura przestrzenna warstw społecznych na Śląsku na tle struktury krajowej" [Spatial structure of social strata in Silesia against the background of the countrywide structure]. Studia Śląskie, New Series 15: 139-50.

Gołębiowski, Bronisław
1974. "Klasy — idee — pokolenia. O ewolucji treści i form sojuszu robotniczo-chłopskiego w Polsce Ludowej" [Classes, ideas, generation. On the evolution of content and forms of the farmer-worker alliance in Poland]. Kultura i Społeczenstwo 18: 55-66.

Graniewska, Danuta
1971. Sytuacja materialna rodzin pracowniczych a zatrudnienie kobiet [Standard of living of families and the employment of women]. Warsaw: Komitet Pracy i Płac.
1975. "Wykształcenie a możliwość karier zawodowych kobiet w Polsce" [Education and career opportunities of Polish women]. Praca i Zabezpieczenie Społeczne 1: 37-40.

Gruber, Katarzyna
1967. "Czynniki społeczne wpływające na wybór zawodu i realizację zamierzen zawodowych młodzieży" [Factors influencing occupational choice and realization of occupational aspirations]. Zeszyty Badania Rejonów Uprzemysławianych 26: 37-82.

Grzelak, Anna
1967. Kariery zawodowe pracowników umysłowych w przemyśle [Occupational careers of nonmanual workers in industry]. Warsaw: C.I.O.P.

Grzelak, Zdzisław
1965. Zależność między studiami a pracą absolwentów szkół wyższych [The relationship between studies and employment of graduates of schools of higher education]. Warsaw: Państwowe Wydawnictwo Naukowe.
1971. Pozycja inteligencji w społeczności wiejskiej [Position of the intelligentsia in villages]. Warsaw: Państwowe Wydawnictwo Naukowe.

Grzeszczyk, Tadeusz
1969. "Awans inżyniera na stanowisko kierownicze w przemyśle" [Advancement of engineers to managerial positions in industry]. Praca i Zabezpieczenie Społeczne 11: 39-42.

Herod, Czesław
1971. "Kształtowanie się składu i struktury społeczno-zawodowej PZDR. Materiały i liczby" [The shaping of the composition and the socio-

occupational structure of the Polish United Workers' Party. Data].
Nowe Drogi 2.
Hochfeld, Julian
   1961. "Marksowska teoria klas: próba systematyzacji" [Marx's theory of
   class: an attempt at systematization]. Studia Socjologiczne 1 and 3.
   1963. Studia o Marksowskiej teorii społeczenstwa [Studies on Marx's theory
   of society]. Warsaw: Państwowe Wydawnictwo Naukowe.
Hryniewicz, Janusz
   1974. "Egalitaryzm a ruchliwość społeczna" [Egalitarism and social mo-
   bility]. Studia Socjologiczne 2(54): 201-16.
Jacukowicz, Zofia
   1972. Relacje płac pracowników umysłowych na podstawie spisu kadrowego
   1968 [Wages of nonmanual workers, based on the 1968 census of employed persons]. Warsaw: Instytut Pracy i Spraw Socjalnych.
   1974. Proporcje płac w Polsce [Wage proportions in Poland]. Warsaw:
   Państwowe Wydawnictwo Ekonomiczne.
Jagiełło-Łysiowa, Eugenia
   1969. Zawód rolnika w świadomości społecznej dwóch pokolen wsi [The occupation of farmer in the social consciousness of two rural genera-
   tions]. Warsaw: Książka i Wiedza.
Jakubczak, Franciszek
   1967. "Pół wieku badan nad rodziną chłopską w Polsce" [Fifty years of research on the peasant family in Poland]. Przegląd Socjologiczny
   22, 2.
Jałowiecki, Bohdan
   1969. "Warunki życia w mieście, wzory zachowan mieszkanców — na przykładzie Lublina" [City living conditions: behavior patterns of the inhabitants of Lublin]. Zeszyty Badan Rejonów Uprzemysławianych
   39: 179-211.
Jałowiecki, Stanisław
   1975. "Miejsce pracy zawodowej w strukturze systemu wartości" [The place
   of occupation in the structure of the value system]. Praca i Zabezpieczenie Społeczne 2: 22-30.
Janicka, Krystyna
   1976. Ruchliwość społeczno-zawodowa i jej korelaty [Socio-occupational
   mobility and its correlates]. Wrocław: Ossolineum.
Janicki, Janusz
   1968. Urzędnicy przemysłowi w strukturze społecznej Polski Ludowej [In-
   dustrial office workers in the social structure of postwar Poland].
   Warsaw: Książka i Wiedza.
Janik, Ryszard, Bolesław Staporek, and Krzysztof Szafnicki
   1970. "Zróżnicowanie społeczne załogi przedsiębiorstwa przemysłowego"
   [Social differentiation in an industrial enterprise]. Studia Socjologiczne 2: 125-46.
Januszkiewicz, Franciszek, and Zofia Kietlinska
   1976. "Czynniki wpływające na systemy rekrutacji na studia wyższe" [Fac-
   tors influencing the systems of recruitment to schools of higher edu-
   cation]. Życie Szkoły Wyższej 5: 77-88.

Bibliography

Jarosinska, Maria
1964. Adaptacja młodzieży wiejskiej do klasy robotniczej [Adaptation of rural youth to the working class]. Wrocław: Ossolineum.
1964. Przystosowanie młodzieży robotniczej do pierwszej pracy [Adaptation of young workers to their first job]. Warsaw: Państwowe Wydawnictwo Naukowe.
1968. Pierwsza praca w opinii dwóch pokolen pracowników [First job in the opinion of two generations of employees]. Warsaw: Ośrodek Badania Opinii Publicznej i Studiów Programowych PRiTV.
1974. "Młodzi robotnicy wobec zawodu i pracy" [Occupation and work of young workers]. Przegląd Związkowy 7-8(299-300): 22-26.
1976. "Badania nad strukturą społeczna w latach 1971-1975" [Research on social structure during the years 1971-1975]. Studia Socjologiczne 3(62): 361-64.
Jędruszczak, Hanna
1971. Zatrudnienie a przemiany społeczne w Polsce 1944-1960 [Employment and social transformations in Poland, 1944-1960]. Wrocław: Ossolineum.
Kaczorowski, Zygmunt
1974. "Rola i pozycja klasy rządzącej" [The role and position of the ruling class]. Przegląd Związkowy 5(297): 43-45.
Kądzielski, Jósef
1963. "Międzypokoleniowa ruchliwość społeczna" [Intergenerational social mobility]. Przegląd Socjologiczny 2.
Kalecki, Michał
1964. "Porównanie dochodu robotników i pracowników umysłowych z okresem przedwojennym" [Comparison of the incomes of workers and non-manual employees with the prewar period]. Kultura i Społeczenstwo 1.
Kassyk, Elżbieta
1975. "Kariery naukowe kobiet" [Scientific careers of women]. Życie Szkoły Wyższej 11: 67-76.
Kawecki, Zenon
1976. "Postawy robotników wobec religii. Z badan nad przemianami w światopoglądzie robotników" [The attitudes of workers toward religion. Research on changes in the world view of workers]. Człowiek i Swiatopogląd 1(126): 71-88.
Kawula, Stanisław
1969. "Aspiracje zawodowe uczniów wiejskich" [Occupational aspirations of students in rural areas]. Wieś Współczesna 13: 109-15.
1976. "Wartości uznawane przez młodzież" [Values accepted by youth]. Przekazy i Opinie 1(3): 19-32.
Kłodzinski, Marek
1974. "Dwuzawodowość w rolnictwie polskim w świetle danych spisu powszechnego z 1970" [Bi-occupational persons in Polish agriculture, based on the 1970 national census]. Wieś i Rolnictwo 1-2: 181-90.
Kłoskowska, Antonina
1969. "Zagadnienia potrzeb i aspiracji kulturalnych środowisk robotniczych" [Problems of cultural needs and aspirations among workers]. Kultura i Społeczenstwo 13: 73-84.

Kobus-Wojciechowska, Anita
1976. Położenie materialne i udział w kulturze [Standard of living and cultural participation]. Wrocław: Ossolineum.
Kochanowski, Tadeusz, and Andrzej Tudek
1974. "Młodzi robotnicy — w swietle badan socjologicznych" [Young workers in the light of sociological research]. Nowe Drogi 8(116): 1-22.
Konopnicki, Jan, ed.
1961. Zainteresowania, środowisko kulturalne, poziom umysłowy młodzieży [Interests, cultural environment, and the mental development of youth]. Wrocław: Ossolineum.
Koralewicz-Zębik, Jadwiga
1974. System wartości a struktura społeczna [The system of values and the social structure]. Wrocław: Ossolineum.
Kordaszewski, Jan
1963. Płaca według pracy. Studium systemu płac w przemyśle [Wages according to work. A study of the wage system in industry]. Warsaw: Książka i Wiedza.
1964. Praca i zatrudnienie w przemyśle [Work and employment in industry]. Warsaw: Panstwowe Wydawnictwo Ekonomiczne.
1969. Pracownicy umysłowi. Dynamika zatrudnienia i metody badania trudności pracy [White-collar workers. Dynamics of employment and methods of investigation of the complexity of work]. Warsaw: Państwowe Wydawnictwo Ekonomiczne.
Kordos, Jan
1968. Metody matematyczne badania i analizy rozkładu dochodów ludności [Mathematical methods in the analysis of the distribution of income]. Warsaw: Główny Urząd Statystyczny.
Kordos, Jan, Barbara Kulczycka, Maryla Pączkowska, and Krzysztof Zagórski
1973. Nowe kadry pracownicze [The new work force]. Warsaw: Główny Urząd Statystyczny.
Kosk, Lidia
1970. "Zawody i płace w gospodarce uspołecznionej" [Occupations and wages in a socialized economy]. Wiadomości Statystyczne 15: 30-34.
1970. "Wykształcenie a płace pracowników w gospodarce uspołecznionej" [Education and wages of employees in a socialized economy]. Wiadomości Statystyczne 15: 32-34.
Kościański, Tadeusz
1966. Studia nad załogami wybranych przedsiębiorstw przemysłowych Lubelszczyzny, 1925-1960 [Studies of employees of selected industrial enterprises of the Lublin region, 1925-1960]. Lublin: Wydawnictwo Lubelskie.
Kowalewska, Salomea
1965. "Definicje i klasyfikacje zawodów" [Definitions and classifications of occupations]. In Adam Sarapata, ed., Socjologia Zawodów. Warsaw: Książka i Wiedza.
Kowalewski, Stanisław
1976. "Egalitaryzacja wykształcenia a integracja środowisk wychowawczych" [Egalitarization of education and integration of educational communi-

Bibliography

ties]. Nauczyciel i Wychowanie 6: 26-38.

Kowalewski, Zdzisław
1962. Chemicy w Polskiej Rzeczypospolitej Ludowej [Chemists in the Polish People's Republic]. Wrocław: Ossolineum.

Kozakiewicz, Mikołaj
1966. "Równy start młodzieży wiejskiej" [Equal opportunity of rural youth]. Wieś Współczesna 10: 76-86.
1968. "Z problematyki awansu społecznego poprzez wykształcenie" [On the problems of social advancement through education]. Wieś Współczesna 12: 42-52.
1976. Skolaryzacja młodzieży polskiej [School attendance of Polish youth]. Warsaw: Państwowe Wydawnictwo Naukowe.
1976. "Rola wykształcenia w procesach ruchliwości społecznej w Polsce" [The role of education in the processes of social mobility in Poland]. Wieś Współczesna 20: 82-91.

Kozakiewicz, Mikołaj, and Zbigniew Kwieciński
1974. "Dostęp młodzieży wiejskiej do kształcenia na różnych szczeblach szkolnictwa" [Access of rural youth to several levels of schooling]. Wieś i Rolnictwo 1-2: 71-100.

Krajewska, Anna
1974. Wykształcenie a zróżnicowanie płac [Education and the differentiation of wages]. Warsaw: Państwowe Wydawnictwo Ekonomiczne.

Krencik, Wiesław
1969. "Rozpiętość płac w przemyśle polskim" [The range of wages in Polish industry]. Gospodarka Planowa 24: 6-11.
1970. "Tendencje zmian struktury płac w gospodarce polskiej" [Trends in the structure of wages in the Polish economy]. Ekonomista 6: 1137-62.
1972. Badanie polityki zatrudnienia i płac w gospodarce socjalistycznej [Investigation of employment policy and wages in a socialized economy]. Warsaw: Państwowe Wydawnictwo Naukowe.

Kryszkiewicz, Stanisław
1976. "Pozycja społeczno-zawodowa mistrza" [Socioeconomic position of foremen]. Nowe Drogi 8(327): 108-18.

Kubiak, Hieronim, and Władysław Kwaśniewicz
1967. "Niektóre aspekty procesu demokratyzacji szkolnictwa wyższego" [Some aspects of the process of democratization in higher education]. Studia Socjologiczne 4: 129-48.

Kulpińska, Jolanta
1969. Aktywność społeczna pracowników przedsiębiorstwa przemysłowego [Social activity of workers in industrial enterprises]. Wrocław: Ossolineum.

Kutyma, Manfred
1974. Progi życiowego sukcesu. Z badań nad wyborem szkoły i zawodu [The threshold of success. Research on the selection of school and occupation]. Warsaw: Państwowe Wydawnictwo Naukowe.

Kwaśniewicz, Władysław
1970. Wiejska społeczność rzemieślnicza w procesie przemian [Rural community of craftsmen in the process of change]. Wrocław: Ossolineum.

1971. "Socjologiczne badania nad makrostruktura w Polsce Ludowej" [Sociological studies on the macrostructure in Poland]. Studia Socjologiczne 4.

Kwiecinski, Zbigniew
1975. "Społeczne zróżnicowanie dróg kształcenia ponadpodstawowego młodzieży. Z badan nad warunkami upowszechniania jednolitej szkoły średniej" [Social differentiation of postelementary education. Research on dissemination of a uniform high school program]. Ruch Pedagogiczny 17: 735-49.

Lipowski, Adam
1966. "Różnice zarobków w gospodarce uspołecznionej Polski w latach 1955-1965" [Wage differences in the socialized economy of Poland, 1955-1965]. Ekonomista 6: 1409-25.

Lutynska, Krystyna
1965. Pozycja społeczna urzędników w Polsce Ludowej [The social position of office workers in Poland]. Wrocław: Ossolineum.

Łach, Wiktor
1965. "Struktura demograficzno-zawodowa społeczności wiejskiej" [The demographic and occupational structure of rural communities]. Kultura i Społeczenstwo 9: 113-28.

Ładosz, Jarosław
1969. "Krytyczne uwagi o metodologii badan struktury społeczenstwa socjalistycznego" [Critical remarks on the methodology of research into the structure of socialist society]. Studia Socjologiczne 2.

Łuc, Kazimierz
1974. "Młodzież wiejska na studiach wyższych" [Rural youth in the schools of higher education]. Wieś Współczesna 18: 124-28.

Machynska, Irena
1970. "Tendencje rozwojowe płac w gospodarce uspołecznionej w Polsce Ludowej" [Trends in wages in the socialized economy of Poland]. Ruch Prawniczy 32: 293-302.

Makarczyk, Wacław
1964. Wyniki badan nad tendencjami migracyjnymi ludności wiejskiej [Research on the migration trends of the rural population]. Łódź: Państwowe Wydawnictwo Naukowe.

1967. "Niektóre problemy badan nad ruchliwością społeczną rolników" [Some problems of research on the social mobility of peasants]. Roczniki Socjologii Wsi 7.

Malanowski, Jan
1962. Robotnicy Warszawskiej Fabryki Motocykli [Workers at the Warsaw motorcycle factory]. Wrocław: Ossolineum.

1967. Stosunki klasowe i różnice klasowe w mieście [Class relationships and social differentiation in a town]. Warsaw: Państwowe Wydawnictwo Naukowe.

1969. "Przemiany w składzie społeczno-zawodowym ludności miejskiej w Polsce w latach 1921-1960" [Changes in the socio-occupational composition of urban populations in Poland, 1921-1960]. In Paweł Rybicki, ed., Społeczno-ludnościowe zagadnienia urbanizacji. Katowice: Śląski Instytut Naukowy.

Bibliography

1973. "Planowanie społeczne a przemiany struktury społecznej" [Social planning and the transformations of social structure]. Wieś Współczesna 17: 91-102.

Malinowski, Roman, and Zenon Mikołajczyk
1965. "Aspiracje i dążenia młodzieży średnich szkół prowincjonalnych" [Aspirations and aims of provincial secondary schools]. Wieś Współczesna 9: 45-57.

Marczyk, Wojciech
1967. "Rola szkoły i nauczyciela w środowisku mobilnym" [The role of schools and teachers in a mobile community]. Zeszyty Badania Rejonów Uprzemysławianych 23: 232-44.
1974. Zainteresowania kulturalne młodych robotników [Cultural interests of young workers]. Warsaw: Instytut Wydawniczy Centralnej Rady Związków Zawodowych.

Marek, Jadwiga
1976. "Kategorie ludności wiejskiej zatrudnionej poza rolnictwem" [Categories of rural population employed outside agriculture]. Zagadnienia Ekonomiki Rolnej 2: 110-17.

Melich, Alojzy
1963. Praca i płaca w przemyśle [Work and wages in industry]. Katowice: Wydawnictwo Śląsk.

Minc, Bronisław
1963. "O rozwarstwieniu społeczenstwa socjalistycznego" [About the stratification of socialist society]. Kultura i Społeczenstwo 3.

Mirowski, Włodzimierz
1968. Migracje do Warszawy. Rola napływu ludności w procesach rozwoju ośrodka wielkomiejskiego. Aktualny skład i czynniki selekcji migrantów [Migrations to Warsaw. The role of population inflow in the development of a metropolitan center. Composition and factors influencing the selection of migrants]. Wrocław: Ossolineum.

Miścicki, Wojciech
1973. Zróżnicowanie społeczne a orientacja ku wartościom [Social differentiation and value orientation]. Wrocław: Ossolineum.

Mleczko, Franciszek
1964. Z badan nad aktywnością zawodową i społeczną chłopów. Studium na przykładzie wsi Łysa Góra [Research on occupational and social activities of farmers. Study of the village Łysa Góra]. Wrocław: Ossolineum.

Mrozek, Wanda
1969. "Rodzina robotnicza w Polsce" [Workers' families in Poland]. In Jan Szczepański, ed., Przemysł i Społeczenstwo w Polsce Ludowej. Wrocław: Ossolineum.
1972. Klasa robotnicza województwa katowickiego w ćwierćwieczu Polski Ludowej [The working class of the Katowice district during twenty-five years of postwar Poland]. Katowice: Śląski Instytut Naukowy, Wydawnictwo Śląsk.

Muszynski, Marek
1976. Transformacja ludności dwuzawodowej [Transformations of the bi-occupational population]. Warsaw: Państwowe Wydawnictwo Naukowe.

Mynarski, Stefan
  1967. Wpływ dochodu i składu osobowego rodziny na wielkość i strukturę jej wydatków [The influence of income and composition of the family on the level and structure of its expenditures]. Wrocław: Ossolineum.
Najduchowska, Halina
  1965. Pozycja społeczna starych robotników przemysłu metalowego [The social position of older workers in the metal industry]. Wrocław: Ossolineum.
  1975. "Preferencje wartości dotyczących przyszłej pracy" [Value preferences pertaining to future work]. Studia Socjologiczne 2(57): 181-94.
Narojek, Winicjusz
  1975. "Przeobrażenia społeczne i perspektywy losu jednostki" [Social transformations from the perspective of individual career]. Studia Socjologiczne 3(58): 63-92.
Nawrocki, Witold
  1976. Klasa, ideologia, literatura [Social class, ideology, and literature]. Poznań: Wydawnictwo Poznanskie.
Neyman, Elżbieta and Zbigniew Tyszka
  1967. "Zróżnicowanie kulturalne a rozwarstwienie społeczne małego miasta" [Social differentiation and stratification in a small town]. Studia Socjologiczne 2: 107-36.
Niezgoda, Marian
  1975. Społeczne determinanty wyboru zawodu [Social determinants of occupational choice]. Wrocław: Ossolineum.
Niklas, Dariusz
  1976. "Zróżnicowania społeczne mowy" [Social differentiation of speech]. Przekazy i Opinie 3(5): 37-50.
Nowak, Irena
  1968. Wzory i normy życia towarzyskiego mieszkanców Warszawy [Patterns and norms of social life of the inhabitants of Warsaw]. Warsaw: Osrodek Badania Opinii Publicznej i Studiów Programowych PRiTV.
  1973. "Struktura społeczna a postawy" [Social structure and attitudes]. In Stefan Nowak, ed., Teorie Postaw. Warsaw: Państwowe Wydawnictwo Naukowe.
Nowak, Marian
  1976. "Społeczne i przestrzenne zróżnicowanie dostępu do oświaty w województwie płockim" [Social and spatial differentiation of the access to education in the Płock region]. Wieś i Rolnictwo 4(13): 101-10.
Nowak, Stefan
  1966. "Psychologiczne aspekty przemian struktury społecznej i ruchliwości społecznej" [Psychological aspects of change in social structure and mobility]. Studia Socjologiczne 2.
Nowakowa, Irena
  1973. Robotnicy w uprzemysławiającym się mieście [Workers in a city in the process of industrialization]. Warsaw: Książka i Wiedza.
Nowakowska, Irena
  1970. "Struktura społeczna młodzieży szkolnej" [Social structure of school students]. Kultura i Społeczenstwo 14: 139-57.

Bibliography

1970. "Kształcenie średnie a struktura społeczna" [Secondary education and social structure]. Nowe Drogi 24: 21-29.

Nowakowski, Stefan
1960. Przeobrażenia społeczne wsi opolskiej [Social change in a village near Opole]. Poznan: Wydawnictwo Poznanskie.
1967. Narodziny miasta [Birth of a town]. Warsaw: Państwowe Wydawnictwo Naukowe.
1975. "Zmiany w makrostrukturze społecznej i ich wpływ na społeczności lokalne miast i wsi" [Changes in the macrostructure of the society and their influence on the local communities of towns and villages]. Kultura i Społeczenstwo 19: 89-104.
1976a. "Pamiętnikarstwo a klasa robotnicza — kultura" [Diaries and the working class culture]. Kultura i Społeczenstwo 20: 53-66.
1976b. "Struktura społeczno-zawodowa większych miast w Polsce" [Socio-occupational structure of large towns in Poland]. Kultura i Społeczenstwo 20: 37-58.

Ohme, Jerzy
1975. Formowanie się załogi zakładu przemysłowego [Development of the work force in an industrial enterprise]. Warsaw: Państwowe Wydawnictwo Naukowe.

Olędzki, Michał
1967. "Ruchliwość zawodowa pracowników Mazowieckich Zakłodów Rafineryjnych i Petrochemicznych w Płocku" [Occupational mobility of employees of the Mazovian refinery and petrochemical plant in Płock]. Biuletyn Instytutu Gospodarstwa Społecznego 10: 43-70.
1967. "Ruchliwość społeczna mieszkanców wsi w okresie wzmożonej industrializacji Płocka" [Social mobility of village inhabitants during increased industrialization of Płock]. Wieś Współczesna 11: 59-70.

Osinski, Jan
1971. Społeczno-przestrzenne uwarunkowania dostępności wyższego wykształcenia [Social and geographic influences on the accessibility of higher education]. Wrocław: Ossolineum.

Ossowski, Stanisław
1957. Struktura klasowa w społecznej świadomości [Class structure in social consciousness]. Łódź: Państwowe Wydawnictwo Naukowe.
1968. Z zagadnien struktury społecznej [Problems of social structure]. Warsaw: Państwowe Wydawnictwo Naukowe.

Paduszek, Jerzy
1969. "Rola szkół srednich w ruchliwości społecznej na przykładzie Radomia" [The role of secondary schools in social mobility, based on data from the city of Radom]. Kultura i Społeczenstwo 13: 181-96.

Pałaszewska-Reindl, Teresa
1966. Konsumpcja dóbr trwałego użytku w Polsce [Consumption of durable goods in Poland]. Warsaw: Państwowe Wydawnictwo Ekonomiczne.

Paszke, Henryk
1976. "Kształtowanie się klasy robotniczej w koninskim rejonie uprzemysłowionym" [The shaping of the working class in the industrialized region of Konin]. Zeszyty Badania Rejonów Uprzemysławianych 65: 139-54.

Pawełczynska, Anna
  1969. Studia nad czytelnictwem [Studies on reading habits]. Warsaw:
        Państwowe Wydawnictwo Naukowe.
Pawlikowska, Krystyna
  1975. "Z zagadnien ruchliwości społecznej" [Problems of social mobility].
        Polityka Społeczna 10(22): 24-27.
Peuker, Zygmunt
  1969. "Zatrudnienie pracowników posiadających tytuły zawodowe i stopnie
        naukowe" [Employment of persons with occupational titles and learned
        degrees]. Wiadomości Statystyczne 14: 23-24.
Piasny, Janusz
  1970. "Podstawowe zmiany w poziomie i strukturze konsumpcji w Polsce
        Ludowej" [Basic changes in the level and structure of consumption in
        Poland]. Ruch Prawniczy 32: 271-91.
Pietraszek, Edward
  1967. "Zróżnicowanie międzywioskowe jako problem struktury społecznej"
        [Intervillage differentiation as a problem of social structure].
        Roczniki Socjologii Wsi 7: 126-35.
  1969. "Typy środowisk robotniczych a ich zróżnicowanie kulturowe" [Vari-
        ous types of worker environments and their cultural differentiation].
        Kultura i Społeczenstwo 13: 105-20.
Podgórecki, Adam
  1976. "Osobowość Polaka a struktura społeczna" [Personality patterns of
        Poles and social structure]. Odra 2: 3-12.
Podgrodzki, Bronisław
  1967. "Swiadomość społeczna wybranej grupy robotników" [Social conscious-
        ness of a selected group of workers]. Biuletyn Sląskiego Instytutu
        Naukowego 73: 5-108.
  1969. Aktywność społeczno-polityczna środowisk robotniczych w województ-
        wie katowickim [Sociopolitical activities among workers in the Kato-
        wice district]. Katowice: Sląski Instytut Naukowy.
Podsiadły, Jerzy
  1968. "Młodzież chłopska na Uniwersytecie Marii Curie-Skłodowskiej" [Ru-
        ral youth at the Maria Curie-Skłodowska University]. Wieś Współ-
        czesna 12: 112-17.
Pohoski, Michał
  1963. Migracja ze wsi do miast [Migrations to cities from rural areas].
        Warsaw: Państwowe Wydawnictwo Ekonomiczne.
  1968. Prestiż zawodów wśród ludności wiejskiej [Occupational prestige
        among the rural population]. Warsaw: Ośrodek Badania Opinii Pub-
        licznej i Studiów Programowych PRiTV.
Pohoski, Michał, Kazimierz Słomczyński, and Krystyna Milczarek
  1974. Standaryzacja zmiennych socjologicznych. T. 2. Społeczna klasyfi-
        kacja zawodów [Standardization of sociological variables. Vol. 2.
        Social classification of occupations]. Warsaw: Instytut Filozofii i
        Socjologii Polskiej Akademii Nauk.
Pomian, Grażyna, and Michał Strzeszewski
  1969. Postawy wobec pracy i zakładu pracy [Attitudes toward work and place

Bibliography

of employment]. Warsaw: Ośrodek Badania Opinii Publicznej i Studiów Programowych PRiTV.

Preiss, Anna

1967a. "Badania losów absolwentów szkół płockich" [Careers of the graduates of the Płock schools]. Zeszyty Badania Rejonów Uprzemysławianych 22: 128-64.

1967b. "Robotnicy a pracownicy inżynieryjno-techniczni" [Workers versus engineers and technicians]. Socjologiczne Problemy Przemysłu i Klasy Robotniczej 2: 19-42.

1976. Technicy — robotnicy w zakładach przemysłowych [Workers and technicians in industrial firms]. Warsaw: Instytut Wydawniczy Centralnej Rady Związków Zawodowych.

Preiss-Zajdowa, Anna

1967. Zawód a praca kobiet [Occupation and employment of women]. Warsaw: Instytut Wydawniczy Centralnej Rady Związków Zawodowych.

Przedpełski, Mieczysław

1975. Struktura zatrudnienia kobiet w Polsce Ludowej [The structure of employment of women in Poland]. Warsaw: Państwowe Wydawnictwo Naukowe.

Rajkiewicz, Antoni

1965. Zatrudnienie w Polsce Ludowej w latach 1950-1970 [Employment in Poland, 1950-1970]. Warsaw: Książka i Wiedza.

Rejnhard-Misiunia, Małgorzata

1976. "Społeczno-zawodowe uwarunkowania opinii o dobrym życiu" [Socio-occupational conditioning of opinions about desirable patterns of living]. Wieś Współczesna 20: 133-37.

Remer, Tadeusz

1976. "Wpływ ruchliwości międzypokoleniowej na ocenę pozycji społecznej" [Influence of intergenerational mobility on evaluation of social position]. Studia Socjologiczne 2(62): 195-217.

Reszke, Irena

1972. Społeczne uwarunkowania wyboru szkoły zawodowej i odpływ uczniów ze szkół [Social conditioning of the selection of trade school and the outflow of students]. Wrocław: Ossolineum.

Rowinski, Leon

1976. "Niektóre uwarunkowania powodzenia w wyższych studiach technicznych" [Some conditions of success in advanced technical training]. Dydaktyka Szkoły Wyższej 1(33): 25-75.

Rutkowski, Wiktor

1975. "Czynniki kształtujące kwalifikacyjno-zawodową strukturę zatrudnienia" [Factors shaping the occupational structure of employment]. Gospodarka Planowa 1(347): 31-33.

Sarapata, Adam

1964. "Niektóre zagadnienia ruchliwości społecznej w badaniach nad klasą robotniczą w Polsce" [Some issues of social mobility in research on the working class in Poland]. Studia Socjologiczne 1.

Sarapata, Adam, ed.

1965a. Przemiany społeczne w Polsce Ludowej [Social change in the Polish

People's Republic]. Warsaw: Państwowe Wydawnictwo Naukowe.

1965b. "Klasa robotnicza w Polsce Ludowej" [The working class in postwar Poland]. In Adam Sarapata, ed., Przemiany spoleczne w Polsce Ludowej. Warsaw: Książka i Wiedza, 471-504.

1965. Studia nad uwarstwieniem i ruchliwością społeczną w Polsce [Studies on social stratification and mobility in Poland]. Warsaw: Książka i Wiedza.

1966. "Z badan nad przemianami w hierarchii zawodów" [Research on changes in the occupational hierarchy]. Studia Socjologiczne 2: 35-52.

1975. "Z badan nad hierarchią prestiżu zajęć w Polsce" [Research on the prestige hierarchy of jobs in Poland]. Studia Socjologiczne 1.

Sękowski, Stanisław

1976. "Problematyka uwarunkowan uczestnictwa w kulturze w badaniach polskich" [Problems of cultural participation in Polish empirical research]. Studia Socjologiczne 4(63): 5-43.

Sianko, Anna

1966. "Wybór zawodu a wzory awansu społecznego młodzieży wiejskiej" [Occupational choice and patterns of social advancement of rural youth]. Studia Socjologiczne 3: 49-64.

Siciński, Andrzej

1962. "Postawy wobec pracy i własności oraz ich społeczne uwarunkowania" [Attitudes toward work and property and their social determinants]. Studia Socjologiczne 2: 64-86.

Sikorska, Joanna

1976. "Wykształcenie jako zmienna różnicująca wzory spożycia" [Education as a variable which differentiates the patterns of consumption]. Studia Socjologiczne 2(61): 237-61.

Słomczyński, Kazimierz

1972. Zróżnicowanie społeczno-zawodowe i jego korelaty [Socio-occupational differentiation and its correlates]. Wrocław: Ossolineum.

Słomczyński, Kazimierz, and Włodzimierz Wesołowski, eds.

1973. Struktura i ruchliwość społeczna [Social structure and mobility]. Wrocław: Ossolineum.

1974. "Aktualne aspekty badań nad strukturą klasową w Polsce" [Some aspects of research on class structure in Poland]. Kultura i Społeczenstwo 18: 115-21.

1976. "Kierunki przemian struktury klasowej" [Directions of transformation of the class structure]. Nowe Drogi 11(330): 43-51.

Socha, Janusz

1968. "Młodzież chłopska a struktura społeczna studentów uczelni łódzkich" [Rural youth and the social structure of students in the schools of higher education in Łódź]. Wieś Współczesna 12: 117-21.

Sochaczewski, Stanisław

1970. "Porównanie sytuacji materialnej robotniko-chłopów i robotników miejskich" [Comparison of the standard of living of peasant-workers with city workers]. Wieś Współczesna 14: 114-19.

Sokołowska, Magdalena, and Krystyna Wrochno

1965. "Pozycja społeczna kobiet w świetle statystyki" [The social position of women, based on statistical data]. Studia Socjologiczne 1: 131-59.

Bibliography

Stachnik, Stanisława
1973. "Problematyka awansu zawodowego pracowników umysłowych" [Problems of occupational advancement of white-collar workers]. Humanizm Pracy 1: 35-43.
Stasiak, Andrzej
1976. "Przemiany demograficzno-społecznej struktury wsi polskiej" [Transformations of the sociodemographic structure of Polish villages]. Wieś Współczesna 20: 58-70.
Stojak, Antoni
1964. Studium o górnikach kopalni "Janina" w Libiążu, 1905-1960 [A study on miners in the "Janina" mine in Libiąż, 1905-1960]. Wrocław: Ossolineum.
Strzemińska, Helena
1969. "Poziom wykształcenia a budżet czasu" [Educational level and the time budget]. Studia i Materiały Instytutu Pracy 53: 57-89.
Strzeszewski, Michał
1971. Materialny poziom życia i jego odbicie w opinii wybranych grup zawodowych [Standard of living reflected in opinions of selected occupational groups]. Warsaw: Ośrodek Badania Opinii Publicznej i Studiów Programowych PRiTV.
Sufin, Zbigniew
1970. "Procesy ruchliwości społecznej" [Processes of social mobility]. In Włodzimierz Wesołowski, ed., Struktura i Dynamika Społeczeństwa Polskiego. Warsaw: Państwowe Wydawnictwo Naukowe.
Surmaczyński, Marian
1966. "Robotnicy w organach władzy państwowej i instancjach partyjnych średniego szczebla" [Workers in middle-level state and party organization]. In Socjologiczne Problemy Przemysłu i Klasy Robotniczej 1: 79-101.
Suszek, Kazimierz
1971. Społeczne podłoże aspiracji szkolnych młodzieży [Social background and the educational aspirations of young people]. Poznań: Państwowe Wydawnictwo Naukowe.
Świrydowicz, Grażyna
1968. "Zawód wyuczony a zawód wykonywany przez absolwentów szkół wyższych" [The occupation learned versus the job held by graduates of schools of higher education]. Życie Szkoły Wyższej 16: 75-82.
Szczepański, Jan
1957. Inteligencja i społeczeństwo [Intelligentsia and society]. Warsaw: Książka i Wiedza.
1965. "Zmiany w strukturze klasowej społeczeństwa polskiego" [Changes in the class structure of Polish society]. In Adam Sarapata, ed., Przemiany Społeczne w Polsce Ludowej. Warsaw: Państwowe Wydawnictwo Naukowe.
1967. "O metodzie przewidywania składu i struktur grup społecznych" [On a method of forecasting the composition and structures of social groups]. Kultura i Społeczeństwo 11: 97-102.
1968. "Przewidywanie uwarstwienia społeczeństwa polskiego w 1985 r."

[Forecasting the stratification of Polish society in 1985]. Kultura i Społeczeństwo 12: 38-42.

1971. Odmiany czasu teraźniejszego [Presentday transformations]. Warsaw: Książka i Wiedza.

1973. Zmiany społeczeństwa polskiego w procesie uprzemysłowienia [Changes in Polish society during the process of industrialization]. Warsaw: Instytut Wydawniczy Centralnej Rady Związków Zawodowych.

1974. "Niektóre cechy rozwoju klasy robotniczej w trzydziestoleciu Polski Ludowej" [Some characteristics of the development of working class in three decades of postwar Poland]. Nauka Polska 6(114): 33-39.

Szczepański, Jan, ed.

1958. Z badań klasy robotniczej i inteligencji [From studies of the working class and intelligentsia]. Łódź: Państwowe Wydawnictwo Naukowe.

1959. Wykształcenie i pozycja społeczna inteligencji [Education and social position of the intelligentsia], vol. 1 (vol. 2, 1960). Łódź: Państwowe Wydawnictwo Naukowe.

1961a. Studia nad rozwojem klasy robotniczej [Studies on the development of the working class]. Warsaw: Państwowe Wydawnictwo Naukowe.

1961b. Studia nad rozwojem klasy robotniczej [Studies on the development of the working class], vol. 1 (vol. 2, 1962). Łódź: Państwowe Wydawnictwo Naukowe.

1974. Narodziny socjalistycznej klasy robotniczej [The birth of the socialist working class]. Warsaw: Instytut Wydawniczy Centralnej Rady Związków Zawodowych.

Szczytowska-Serafinowicz, Danuta

1970. "Aktywność zawodowa kobiet" [Occupational activities of women]. Wiadomości Statystyczne 15: 24-26.

Szostkiewicz, Stefan

1965. Przemiany w strukturze załogi Fabryki Samochodów Osobowych [Changes in the work force structure of the passenger motorcar factory]. Wrocław: Ossolineum.

Sztumski, Janusz

1969. "Załoga przedsiębiorstwa przemysłowego w ujęciu socjologii" [Employees of an industrial enterprise seen in a sociological framework]. Ruch Prawniczy 31: 269-80.

1976. "Pieniądz w świetle socjologii — społeczne funkcje pieniądza" [Money in the light of sociology. The social functions of money]. Studia Socjologiczne 1(60): 89-100.

Tarkowski, Jacek, Jerzy Wiatr, and Krzysztof Zagórski

1972. Radni i członkowie prezydiów rad narodowych, 1958-1968 [Counselors and members of presidiums of people's councils, 1958-1968]. Warsaw: Główny Urząd Statystyczny.

Tobera, Piotr

1972. Zróżnicowanie społeczne pracowników przemysłu [Social differentiation of industrial workers]. Warsaw: Państwowe Wydawnictwo Naukowe.

Tokarska, Irena

1974. "Aspiracje zawodowe uczniów klas ósmych" [Occupational aspirations of eighth-grade students]. Kwartalnik Pedagogiczny 1(71): 153-63.

Bibliography

Turczyn-Zioło, Irma, and Zbigniew Zioło
1976. "Zróżnicowanie struktury zawodowej tarnobrzeskiego ośrodka miejskiego i jego zaplecza rolniczego" [Differentiation of occupational structure in the Tarnobrzeg urban center and its agricultural supply areas]. Zeszyty Rejonów Uprzemysławianych 64: 35-79.

Turowski, Jan
1965. Przemiany tradycyjnej wiejskiej społeczności lokalnej w Polsce [Changes in the traditional rural local community in Poland]. Roczniki Socjologii Wsi 4: 17-39.

Turowski, Jan, and Piotr Kryczka
1970. "Struktury społeczne 'starego' i nowego miasta przemysłowego" [Social structures of an "old" and a new industrial city]. In Jan Turowski, ed., Studia Socjologiczne i Urbanistyczne Miast Lubelszczyzny. Lublin: Wydawnictwo Lubelskie.

Turski, Ryszard
1965. Między miastem i wsią [Between city and village]. Warsaw: Państwowe Wydawnictwo Naukowe.
1967. "Z problematyki ruchliwości społecznej w środowisku wiejskim" [Some problems of social mobility in a village]. Roczniki Socjologii 7: 13-56.
1969. "Przemysł a przemiany wsi" [Industry and the transformation of rural areas]. In Jan Szczepański, ed., Przemysł a Społeczeństwo w Polsce Ludowej. Wrocław: Ossolineum.
1970. "Przemiany struktury społecznej wsi" [Changes in social structure in rural areas]. In Włodzimierz Wesołowski, ed., Struktura i Dynamika Społeczeństwa Polskiego. Warsaw: Państwowe Wydawnictwo Naukowe.

Tymowski, Andrzej
1967. "Dochody i wydatki pracowników fizycznych i umysłowych" [Incomes and expenditures of manual and nonmanual workers]. Kultura i Społeczeństwo 11: 195-203.
1970. "Pochodzenie a warunki bytu rodziny" [Social origins and the standard of living of families]. Studia Socjologiczne 2: 147-66.
1973. Minimum socjalne, metodyka i próba określenia [Minimal standard of living. Methods and an attempt at definition]. Warsaw: Państwowe Wydawnictwo Naukowe.

Tyszka, Andrzej
1971. Uczestnictwo w kulturze [Participation in culture]. Warsaw: Państwowe Wydawnictwo Naukowe.

Tyszka, Zbigniew
1970. Przeobrażenia rodziny robotniczej w warunkach uprzemysłowienia i urbanizacji. Studium socjologiczne oparte na badaniach w uprzemysławianym rejonie konińskim [Transformations of workers' families under the influence of industrialization and urbanization. A sociological study based on research in the industrial region of Konin]. Warsaw: Państwowe Wydawnictwo Naukowe.
1971. Rodzina a zakład pracy [The family and the place of work]. Warsaw: Wydawnictwo Związkowe Centralnej Rady Związków Zawodowych.

Wasiak, Kazimierz
1976. "Poglądy szczecińskiej młodzieży robotniczej na rolę klas społecznych" [Opinions of working class youth in Szczecin about the role
of social classes]. Kultura i Społeczeństwo 20: 125-42.
Wasilewski, Jacek
1976. "Stan zatrudnienia i struktura załogi Huty im. Lenina — tendencje
zmian w ostatnich latach" [Employees and the structure of employment of Lenin foundry works; changes in recent years]. Zeszyty Naukowe Uniwersytetu Jagiellońskiego. Prace Socjologiczne 3: 75-86.
Warzywoda-Kruszyńska, Wielisława
1974. Małżeństwa a struktura społeczna [Marriage and social structure].
Wrocław: Ossolineum.
Wesołowski, Włodzimierz
1966. Klasy, warstwy i władza [Classes, strata, and power]. Warsaw:
Państwowe Wydawnictwo Naukowe.
1969. "Przemiany strukturalne w socjaliźmie" [Structural transformation
in socialism]. Studia Socjologiczne 2: 43-62.
1971. "Planowanie i prognozowanie przemian struktury klasowej" [Planning
and forecasting of class structure transformations]. Studia Nauk Poli-
tycznych 1.
1975a. Teoria, badania, praktyka: z problematyki struktury klasowej [The-
ory, research, praxis: Problems of class structure]. Warsaw:
Książka i Wiedza.
1975b. Młodzi robotnicy. Kwalifikacje, postawy, aspiracje [Young workers:
Qualifications, attitudes, and aspirations]. Warsaw: Instytut Wydawniczy Centralnej Rady Związków Zawodowych.
Wesołowski, Włodzimierz, ed.
1970. Zróżnicowanie społeczne [Social differentiation]. Wrocław: Ossolineum.
1974. Standaryzacja zmiennych socjologicznych. T. 1. Wiek, wykształcenie, dochód, sytuacja mieszkaniowa [Standardization of sociological
variables. Vol. 1. Age, education, income, and housing standards].
Warsaw: Instytut Filozofii i Socjologii Polskiej Akademii Nauk.
Wesołowski, Włodzimierz, and Adam Sarapata
1961. "Hierarchia zawodów i stanowisk" [The hierarchy of occupations and
positions]. Studia Socjologiczne 2: 85-115.
Wesołowski, Włodzimierz, and Jadwiga Koralewicz-Zębik
1969. "Przemiany struktury klasowej i warstwowej w Polsce" [Transfor-
mations of the class and stratum structure in Poland]. In Jan Szczepański, ed., Przemysł i Społeczeństwo w Polsce Ludowej. Wrocław:
Ossolineum.
Wesołowski, Włodzimierz, and Jan Błuszkowski
1975. "Ewolucja struktury społecznej w Polsce Ludowej" [Evolution of social structure in Poland]. Nowe Drogi 12(319): 57-70.
Wiatr, Jerzy
1962. "Uwarstwienie społeczne a tendencje egalitarne" [Social stratification and egalitarian tendencies]. Kultura i Społeczeństwo 2: 35-58.

Bibliography

1965. "Inteligencja w Polsce Ludowej" [The intelligentsia in Poland]. In
Adam Sarapata, ed., Przemiany Społeczne w Polsce Ludowej. Warsaw:
Państwowe Wydawnictwo Naukowe.

1967. "Istota sporu wokół stratyfikacji społecznej" [The essence of disputes
about social stratification]. Nowe Drogi 21: 28-36.

1971. "Polityczne następstwa przemian struktury społecznej" [Political
effects of change in the social structure]. Nowe Drogi 1: 82-106.

Widerszpil, Stanisław
1965. Skład polskiej klasy robotniczej [The composition of the Polish working class]. Warsaw: Państwowe Wydawnictwo Naukowe.

1965. "Interpretacja przemian struktury społecznej w Polsce Ludowej" [In-
terpretation of changes in the social structure in postwar Poland].
Nowe Drogi 1: 60-72.

1973. Przeobrażenia struktury społecznej w Polsce Ludowej [The transformation of the social structure in postwar Poland]. Warsaw: Książka
i Wiedza.

Widerszpil, Stanisław, and Janusz Janicki
1959. "Do jakiej klasy należysz?" [To what social class do you belong?].
Życie Gospodarcze 25, 27.

Wieruszewski, Roman
1975. Równość kobiet i mężczyzn w Polsce Ludowej [Equality of men and
women in Poland]. Poznań: Wydawnictwo Poznańskie.

Wierzbicki, Zbigniew
1976. "Rozwój świadomości narodowej chłopów polskich" [Development of
national consciousness of Polish farmers]. Studia Socjologiczne 2:
169-93.

Wierzchowski, Jerzy
1976. "Uwarunkowania społeczne uczestnictwa w kulturze młodzieży szkolnej" [Social conditions for participation in culture of school youth].
Wieś Współczesna 20: 44-51.

Wnuk-Lipiński, Edmund
1972. Praca i wypoczynek w budżecie czasu [Work and recreation in the
time budget]. Wrocław: Ossolineum.

Wojtaszek, Jan
1966. "Struktura klasowa w świadomości społecznej" [Class structure in
the social consciousness]. Socjologiczne Problemy Przemysłu i
Klasy Robotniczej 1: 177-98.

Wojtyniak, Bogdan
1975. "Niektóre cechy demograficzno-społeczne ludności napływowej za-
mieszkałej w Krakowie" [Certain sociodemographic characteristics
of immigrants living in Cracow]. Studia Demograficzne 39: 145-55.

Wyderko, Adam
1969. "Zmiany w zarobkowaniu na wsi w latach 1962-1967" [Changes in
earnings in the villages, 1962-1967]. Zagadnienia Ekonomiki Rolnej
25: 96-101.

Zagórski, Krzysztof
1969. Społeczne zróżnicowanie ocen sytuacji materialnej [Social differentiation in the evaluations of the standard of living]. Warsaw: Ośrodek

Badania Opinii Publicznej i Studiów Programowych PRiTV.

1970. "Warunki materialno-bytowe robotników i inteligencji" [The standard of living of workers and the intelligentsia]. In Włodzimierz Wesołowski, ed., Struktura i Dynamika Społeczeństwa Polskiego. Warsaw: Państwowe Wydawnictwo Naukowe.

1974. "Zmiany w strukturze i ruchliwości społecznej w Polsce" [Changes in social structure and mobility in Poland]. Wiadomości Statystyczne 5.

1976. Zmiany struktury i ruchliwość społeczno-zawodowa w Polsce [Changes of structure and socio-occupational mobility in Poland]. Warsaw: Główny Urząd Statystyczny.

Zagórski, Krzysztof, and Wiesław Bielicki

1966. Robotnicy wczoraj i dziś [Workers yesterday and today]. Warsaw: Wiedza Powszechna.

Ziobro, Henryk

1965. "Uczestnictwo w życiu kulturalnym młodzieży pochodzenia chłopskiego" [Participation in culture by young people from a farming background]. Studia Pedagogiczne 13: 158-98.

Żekoński, Zygmunt, and Irena Żukowska

1968. "Analiza koncentracji płac, dochodów i wydatków" [An analysis of concentration of wages, incomes, and expenditures]. Gospodarka Planowa 23: 8-14.

Żygulski, Kazimierz

1964. Wybór i poważanie zawodów na Śląsku [The choice and prestige of occupations in Silesia]. Wrocław: Ossolineum.

ABOUT THE EDITORS

Kazimierz Słomczyński, a prominent Polish sociologist and the author and editor of several major books on social mobility in Poland, is the Scientific Director of the Institute of Sociology at the University of Warsaw.

Tadeusz Krauze, author of numerous articles on the sociology of science, was born in Poland. He spent 1976-78 in Cornell's program on social analyses of science systems and is now Assistant Professor of Sociology at Hofstra University.

Murray Yanowitch is the author of Social and Economic Inequality in the Soviet Union and co-editor, with Wesley Fisher, of Social Stratification and Mobility in the USSR.